THE MEANS O

OF THE PHYSICAL AND MORAL QUALITIES

OF ALLAH'S MESSENGER

THE MEANS OF ARRIVING AT KNOWLEDGE OF THE PHYSICAL AND MORAL QUALITIES OF ALLAH'S MESSENGER

Wasāʾil al-Wusūl ilā Shamāʾil al-Rasūl ﷺ

SHAYKH YŪSUF B. ISMĀʿĪL
AL-NABAHĀNĪ

TRANSLATED BY ABDUL AZIZ SURAQAH

The Means of Arriving at Knowledge
Of the Physical and Moral Qualities of Allah's Messenger ﷺ

ISBN: 978-0-9900026-8-0
Published by: Al Madina Institute
www.almadinainstitute.org

Translated by Abdul Aziz Suraqah
Edited by Abdul Aziz Suraqah and Hashem Meriesh
Designed and Typeset by Abdallateef Whiteman
Printed in the United States of America

Contents

CHAPTER FOUR

Translator's Note

ALL PRAISE IS due to Allah by whom all good things come to fruition. May He send infinite prayers and salutations upon our master Muḥammad, the Primordial Prophet of truth sent with truth, and the guide unto the straight path, and upon his Family and Companions.

In rendering this work into English I am indebted to the works of those scholars who penned detailed commentaries on the *Shamāʾil*, most notably Shaykh ʿAbdullāh b. Saʿīd al-Laḥjī's Muntahā al-sūl. All hadith references in this work are taken from his groundbreaking work, and occasionally from the edition of Ibrāhīm Shams al-Dīn (Dar al-Kotob al-ʻIlmiyya, 2002). The text on which this translation is based is the 2002 Dār al-Minhāj edition. For the sake of presenting the cream of this work, we have elected to omit chapters seven and eight (Miscellanea, and Prophetic Medicine). May Allah accept this humble show of love for the Chief of Mankind, our beloved Prophet Muḥammad ﷺ.

ABDUL AZIZ SURAQAH

Biography of Shaykh Yūsuf b. Ismāʿīl al-Nabahānī

HE IS THE erudite scholar and "poet of the Prophet ﷺ," Shaykh Yūsuf b. Ismāʿīl b. Yūsuf b. Ismāʿīl b. Muḥammad Nāṣir al-Dīn al-Nabahānī. Born in the village of Ijzim near Haifa, Palestine in the year 1265 AH (1849 CE), Shaykh Yūsuf al-Nabahānī received a pious upbringing and learned the Quran from his father, the masterful memorizer and reciter Shaykh Ismāʿīl al-Nabahānī, about whom al-Nabahānī said, "My father's daily and nightly litany consisted of reading one third of the Quran, and then later he would complete the Quran three times every week, and all praise is for Allah!"

After memorizing the Quran under the instruction of his father, al-Nabahānī received permission to travel to Cairo, Egypt, where in 1283 AH (1866 CE) he began his formal Islamic studies in the Great Mosque of al-Azhar and remained there until 1289 AH (1872 CE).

He says of himself during this period:

> During that time, I learned all that Allah had decreed for me to learn of the sciences of the Sacred Law and its ancillary disciplines from accomplished and realized Shaykhs and firmly grounded scholars who, if they had set out individually to a region, they would be the leaders of the people to the Gardens of

bliss and would suffice them from needing any others in all of the required sciences ...

HIS TEACHERS

Shaykh Yūsuf al-Nabahānī says of his teachers:

> One of them, or rather their peerless leader, was the singular and erudite master and refuge, the meticulous polymath and Shaykh of Shaykhs and teacher of teachers, my master Shaykh Ibrāhīm al-Saqqā al-Shāfiʿī, who passed away in 1298 AH, aged around ninety years. He spent his long blessed life in teaching, so much that the bulk of the scholars of our time are his students, either directly or through an intermediary. I kept up my lessons with him—may Allah have mercy on him!—for three years and studied under his instruction Shaykh al-Islām Zakariyyā al-Anṣārī's commentary on *al-Taḥrīr* and *al-Minhāj* respectively, both with the glosses of al-Sharqāwī and al-Bujayrimī...
>
> My other teachers included:
>
> The venerable and erudite Sayyid Muḥammad al-Damanhūrī al-Shāfiʿī, who passed away in 1286 AH at around ninety years of age.
>
> My master, the erudite Shaykh Ibrāhīm al-Zurrū al-Khalīlī al-Shāfi, who passed away in 1287 AH at around seventy years old.
>
> The erudite scholar, my master Shaykh Aḥmad al-Ajhūrī al-Ḍarīr al-Shāfiʿī, who passed away in 1293 AH at around sixty years old.

The erudite scholar, my master Shaykh Ḥasan al-ʿAdawī al-Mālikī, who passed away in 1298 AH at around eighty years old.

The erudite scholar, my master Shaykh al-Sayyid ʿAbd al-Hādī Najā al-Abyārī, who passed away in 1305 AH at just over seventy years old.

Shaykh Shams al-Dīn Muḥammad al-Anbābī al-Shāfiʿī, the Master of al-Azhar Mosque, who passed away in 1313 ah.

Shaykh ʿAbd al-Raḥmān al-Shirbīnī al-Shāfiʿī, Master of al-Azhar Mosque, who passed away in 1313 AH.

Shaykh ʿAbd al-Qādir al-Rāfiʿī al-Ḥanafī al-Ṭarābulsī, the master of the Levantine quarters in al-Azhar Mosque, who passed away in 1323 AH.

Shaykh Yūsuf al-Barqāwī al-Ḥanbalī, the master of the Ḥanbalī quarters in al-Azhar Mosque.

And many others, may Allah have mercy upon them all!

SHAYKH YŪSUF AL-NABAHĀNĪ'S CAREER

In the year 1289 AH (1872 CE) after completing his studies at al-Azhar, Shaykh Yūsuf al-Nabahānī returned to his native Palestine, where in Akka he organized lessons teaching the sacred sciences and the Arabic language, and took a position one year later as an assistant judge in Jenin, where he remained until 1293 AH (1876 CE). He then moved to Constantinople, capitol of the Ottoman Caliphate, where he worked on and off for several years as an editor of the Arabic periodical *al-Jawāʾib* and proofread the Arabic works that it published. He then left Constantinople for Iraq, where he settled for five months as a judge in Mosul, and soon resettled in Al-Lādhiqiya and took a position as chief judge in its criminal court. After living there and serving as a judge for five years, Shaykh Yūsuf al-Nabahānī was transferred to Jerusalem and appointed chief judge of its criminal court, where he remained less than a year before being reassigned as chief judge of the criminal court of Beirut in 1305 AH. The Shaykh was to remain as chief judge in Beirut's criminal court until he retired in 1909 CE. After his retirement the Shaykh wrote and published the majority of his books and spent time in the Blessed City of the Prophet ﷺ, Medina, returning to his native Ijzim after the start of World War I in 1914 and remaining there until he passed away in the year 1350 AH (1932 CE).

SHAYKH YŪSUF AL-NABAHĀNĪ'S WRITTEN WORKS

It is without exaggeration to say that Allah gifted Shaykh Yūsuf al-Nabahānī with a flowing pen that was put in service of the august Prophetic station. By the blessings of his love and intimate connection with the Prophet ﷺ and His illustrious Household, Shaykh Yūsuf al-Nabahānī wrote a staggering number of works dedicated to the Prophet, many of which form the curriculum in several traditional Islamic schools and seminaries. His works include:

Afḍal al-ṣalawāt ʿalā Sayyid al-Sādāt (The Most Virtuous Prayers upon the Master of Masters)

Aḥsan al-wasāʾil fī naẓm asmāʾ al-Nabī al-Kāmil (The Best of Means in Versifying the Names of the Perfect Prophet ﷺ

Al-Aḥādīth al-arbaʿin fī faḍl Sayyid al-Mursalīn (Forty Hadith Reports on the Virtues of the Master of the Messengers ﷺ)

Al-Aḥādīth al-arbaʿīn fī faḍl al-jihād wa al-mujāhidīn (Forty Hadith Reports on the Virtue of Jihad and Those Engaged in It)

Al-Aḥādīth al-arbaʿīn fī wujūb ṭāʿat Amīr al-Muʾminīn (Forty Hadith Reports on the Obligation of Rendering Obedience to the Commander of the Believers)

Al-Aḥādīth al-arbaʿīn min amthāl Afsaḥ al-Mursalīn (Forty Hadith Reports Containing Metaphors Uttered by the Most Eloquent of the Messengers ﷺ)

Al-Anwār al-Muḥammadiyya (The Muḥammadan Lights, an abridgment of Imam al-Qasṭalānī's *al-Mawāhib al-laduniyya*)

Al-Arbaʿīn al-arbaʿīn min aḥādīth Sayyid al-Mursalīn (Forty Times Forty Hadith Reports from the Master of the Messengers ﷺ)

Arbaʿūna ḥadīthan fī arbaʿīn ṣīghatin fī al-ṣalāt ʿalā al-Nabī (Forty Hadith Reports on Forty Wordings of Prayers upon the Prophet ﷺ)

Arbaʿūna ḥadīthan fī faḍāʾil Ahl al-Bayt (Forty Hadith Reports on the Virtues of the Prophetic Household)

Arbaʿūna ḥadīthan fī faḍl Abī Bakr رضي الله عنه (Forty Hadith Reports on the Virtue of Abū Bakr رضي الله عنه)

Arbaʿūna ḥadīthan fī faḍl Abī Bakr wa ʿUmar (Forty Hadith Reports on the Virtues of Abū Bakr and ʿUmar رضي الله عنهما)

Arbaʿūna ḥadīthan fī faḍl ʿAlī (Forty Hadith Reports on the Virtue of ʿAli ﷺ)

Arbaʿūna ḥadīthan fī faḍl arbaʿīna Ṣaḥābiyan (Forty Hadith Reports on the Virtue of Forty Companions)

Arbaʿūn ḥadīthan fī faḍl Lā ilāha illā Allāh (Forty Hadith Reports on the Merit of the Phrase "There is no god but Allah")

Arbaʿūna ḥadīthan fī faḍl ʿUmar (Forty Hadith Reports on the Virtue of ʿUmar ﷺ)

Arbaʿūna ḥadīthan fī faḍl ʿUthmān (Forty Hadith Reports on the Virtue of ʿUthmān ﷺ)

Al-Asālīb al-badīʿa fī faḍl al-Ṣaḥāba wa iqnāʿ al-shīʿa (The Marvelous Styles of Detailing the Virtue of the Companions and Persuading the Shiites)

Al-Asmā fī mā li Rasūlillāh ﷺ min al-asmāʾ (The Loftiest Reach Concerning the Names of the Messenger of Allah ﷺ)

Al-Bashāʾir al-īmāniyya fī al-mubasshirāt al-manāmiyya (The Faith-Borne Glad Tidings in Positive Dream Visions)

Al-Burhān al-musaddad fī ithbāt Nubuwwat Sayyidinā Muḥammad ﷺ (The Fortified Demonstrations of the Prophethood of our Master Muḥammad ﷺ)

Dalīl al-tujjār ilā akhlāq al-akhyār (The Guide of the Merchants to the Noble Qualities of the Elect)

Al-Dalālāt al-wāḍiḥāt sharḥ Dalāʾil al-khayrāt (The Clear Indications: Commentary upon *Dalāʾil al-khayrāt*)

Tanbīh al-afkār ilā ḥikmat iqbāl al-dunyā ʿalā al-kuffār (Bringing Attention to the Minds about the Wisdom behind the Disbeliever's Worldly Affluence)

Tahdhīb al-nufūs fī tartib al-durūs (An abridgement of al-Nawawī's *Riyāḍ al-ṣāliḥīn*)

Jāmiʿ karāmāt al-Awliyāʾ (Compendium of the Miracles of the Saints)

Jawāhir al-biḥār fī faḍāʾil al-Nabī al-Mukhtār (The Jewels of the Oceans Concerning the Virtues of the Chosen Prophet ﷺ)

Ḥujjat Allāh ʿalā al-ʿālamīn fī muʿjizāt Sayyid al-Mursalīn (Allah's Proof over all Creation in the Inimitable Miracles of the Master of the Messengers ﷺ)

Riyāḍ al-Janna fī adhkār al-Kitāb wa al-Sunna (Gardens of Paradise in the Invocations of the Quran and Sunna)

Sabīl al-najāt fī al-ḥubb fī Allāh wa al-bughḍ fī Allāh (The Path of Salvation through Loving and Hating for Allah's Pleasure)

Saʿadat al-anām fī ittibāʿ dīn al-Islām wa tawḍīḥ al-farq baynahu wa bayn dīn al-naṣārā fī al-ʿaqāʾid wa al-aḥkām (The Felicity of Humanity Found in Following the Religion of Islam, and a Clarification of the Theological and Legal Differences between it and Christianity)

Saʿādat al-dārayn fī al-ṣalāt ʿalā Sayyid al-Kawnayn (Felicity in the two Abodes in Prayers upon the Master of the Two Realms)

Al-Sharaf al-muʾabbad li Āli Muḥammad (Eternal Honor for the Family of Muḥammad ﷺ)

Shawāhid al-ḥaqq fī al-istighātha bi Sayyid al-Khalq (The Corroborations of Truth Regarding the Act of Seeking Aid from the Master of Creation ﷺ)[1]

1 The main references for this biography come from Sheikh Yūsuf al-Nabahānī's brief autobiography appended to his *Jāmiʿ karāmāt al-Awliyāʾ*, as well as ʿAbd al-Razzāq al-Bayṭār's *Ḥilyat al-bashr fī tārīkh al-qarn al-thālith ʿashr*.

Introduction

PRAISE be to Allah the Lord of the Worlds—a praise in the measure of His blessings and commensurate with His increase of them and matching His generosity. I bear witness that there is no god but Allah, who is the King, the Real, the Manifest, and I bear witness that our master Muḥammad is His servant and Messenger, and the master of all created beings. O Allah! Send the finest, most perfect, most enduring, and most comprehensive of prayers and most abundant of salutations upon our master Muḥammad, Your servant for whom You have selected the rank of universal leadership, and who is thus the liege lord of all worlds; Your Messenger whom You have sent with the best of descriptions and the most persuasive of proofs, that he may perfect the noble qualities of character—a prayer that corresponds to the closeness between You and him which none besides him have attained; a prayer that parallels the love between You and him, which is uniquely his from time immemorial and for all eternity; a prayer that cannot be enumerated or delimited by pen or tongue, nor be described or known by angel or man; a prayer that lieges over all other prayers, just as he lieges over all of creation; a prayer whose light surrounds me from all directions and encompasses all of my moments and remains inseparable from every atom of my being, in my life and after my death—and may prayers and salutations also be upon his pure Family and elect Companions!

It occurred to me that I should compile a work that I could use as a means of attaining Allah's good-pleasure and closeness to His Messenger [ﷺ], and as a way to join the ranks of those who offered sincere service to him, may salutations and prayers be upon him. But then I looked at the paucity of my knowledge and the feebleness of my understanding, and the enormity of my sins and abundance of faults, and I was held back, bridled as a man who knows his limits and stops before going any further. Afterwards, however, I thought of the vast honor of being from the nation of this noble Prophet [ﷺ], so I stepped forward as a baby steps forward to walk towards his compassionate and forbearing father. This was after I heard the words of Allah Most High, "*Certainly there has come to you a Messenger from your own selves. It grieves him that you should suffer. He is keen for your wellbeing, and he is, with the believers, full of pity and compassionate.*" (Quran 9:128) How many a dimwitted Bedouin bereft of propriety, understanding, intellect, knowledge, dignity, and forbearance came to the noble Prophet with what would earn his ire and wrath, and spoke to him in such a way as to make a sword frown and turn tongues into lances, yet the Prophet's response would be to overlook and pardon the wrongdoer—nay, he would even draw such a person near to him, and would not rebuke or upbraid him. Instead, his Muhammadan Character would pour out to that person a drink of the Alchemy of Happiness and give it to him with hands of excellence, till the edge of the man's boorishness was dulled and its steel transformed into a jewel of humanity—his anger being replaced by love, his remoteness replaced by proximity, his war replaced by peace, his ignorance replaced by knowledge, being transformed into a human after having been a serpent, and becoming beloved after having been a wolf!

The above-mentioned, and more, are testimonies to the Prophet's noble qualities of character ﷺ that convinced me that it is within reach to be accepted among his servants and welcomed into the ranks of his retinue. It is not farfetched in the least for Allah's generosity to bestow upon me—out of honor for His Messenger—far beyond my hopes for divine pleasure and acceptance.

Here I place my trust in Him (Exalted is He!) and take a handful from the narrations of the Messenger ﷺ, gathering herein the reports that speak of his noble description and features, and including virtually all of the contents of the *Shamāʾil* collection narrated by the imam and hadith master Abū ʿĪsā Muḥammad b. ʿĪsā al-Tirmidhī (after omitting its repetitions and chains of transmission). I have not limited myself to his arrangement and chapter headings; instead, I chose a style of presentation different from his, and added other narrations from the books of the other imams (whom I shall soon mention), as well as explanations and vowelizations for obscure words when the need arose. And thus this book comes unparalleled, and I have entitled it *The Means of Arrival to Knowledge of the Physical and Moral Qualities of Allah's Messenger* ﷺ.

What follows is a mention of the works from which I have quoted or from which I have narrated:

The *Shamāʾil* of Imam al-Tirmidhī

Al-Maṣābīḥ of Imam al-Baghawī

Iḥyāʾ ʿulūm al-dīn of Imam al-Ghazālī

Al-Shifā of Qāḍī ʿIyāḍ

Tahdhīb al-asmāʾ wa al-lughāt of Imam al-Nawawī

Al-Hadyī al-Nabawī of Imam Muḥammad b. Abī Bakr, better known as Ibn Qayyim al-Jawziyya

Al-Jāmiʿ al-ṣaghīr of Imam al-Suyūṭī

Sharḥ al-Jāmiʿ al-ṣaghīr of Imam al-ʿAzīzī

Al-Mawāhib al-laduniyya of Imam al-Qasṭalānī

Kashf al-ghumma of Imam al-Shaʿrānī

Ṭabaqāt al-Awliyāʾ of Imam al-Munāwī

Kunūz al-ḥaqāʾiq of Imam al-Munāwī

The gloss of the *Shamāʾil,* by the teacher of my teachers, the seal of the practicing scholars, Shaykh Ibrāhīm al-Bājūrī

May Allah be pleased with them all!

THE MEANING OF THE TERM *SHAMĀʾIL*

Linguistically, *shamāʾil* means qualities of character and natures. [Al-Fayrūzabādī] said in *al-Qāmūs,* "[The word] *shimāl* means nature, and its plural is *shamāʾil.*" [Ibn Manẓūr] said in *Lisān al-ʿArab,* "Its singular form is *shimāl,* with a *kasra* vowel mark on the letter *shīn*... *Shimāl* can refer to a person's innate character. Its plural is *shamāʾil*. It is said that a woman has good *shamāʾil,* or a man has noble *shamāʾil,* if they have good qualities of character and good relations with others."

The scholars of hadith use the word *shamāʾil* primarily to refer to the Prophet's noble qualities of character, and secondarily and figuratively to refer to his outer form. Understand this.

THE BENEFITS THAT ARE SOUGHT AFTER IN COMPILING THE *SHAMĀʾIL*

The purpose of gathering the descriptions of the Prophet ﷺ is not merely for the sake of knowing history to which souls incline and hearts turn, or to be used as a conversation piece in gatherings, or to be used for other motives. The objective behind the compilation of the Prophet's descriptions is to attain important religious benefits. These include: taking delight and enjoyment in his lofty attributes and well-pleasing descriptions ﷺ and drawing close to him and engendering his love and good pleasure by mentioning his perfect qualities and virtuous character traits, just as a poet draws near to a noble patron by mentioning his beautiful qualities and noble features. There is no doubt that compiling the Prophet's descriptions and disseminating them is superior and better than praising him through odes. The Prophet ﷺ was pleased with those who praised him in poetry, such as Ḥassān [b. Thābit], ʿAbdullāh b. Abī Rawāḥa, and Kaʿb b. Zuhayr—he was pleased with them and compensated them for their poetry, so there is no doubt that he is also well pleased with those who show great concern in compiling and disseminating his descriptions ﷺ.

Another benefit of compiling the Prophet's descriptions is that by doing so we are in a position to give in return for his excellence towards us ﷺ and his having delivered us from the dark shadows of misguidance and lead us to the lights of guidance, and for his having saved us from eternal damnation and lead us to eternal felicity. This is a supreme grace that cannot be paid back with anything, and none can give to him in full measure except Allah Most High—"so may Allah reward him on our behalf with the best that one has ever given his envoy, for through him Allah has saved us from destruction and made us the best nation that has arisen among mankind, with us holding as our religion the way of life that He has chosen for us, and which He chose for His angels and those He has blessed from His creation. Thus no grace, whether open or hidden, has come to us, and by which we have obtained good fortune in our religious or worldly matters or by which misfortune has been lifted from one or both of them [the religious or the worldly matters], except that Muḥammad ﷺ is the cause thereof, and the one who has lead us to its goodness and guided us to the best of it."[1]

Another benefit of compiling the Prophet's noble descriptions is that it engenders love for him ﷺ. That is because man is predisposed to love beautiful qualities and the one described with them; and there are no qualities more beautiful and more perfect than the Prophet's ﷺ, so there is no doubt whatsoever that anyone who examines them—so long as his heart is not sealed with a seal of misguidance—will love the one who possesses them ﷺ with certitude. Without doubt, the increase and decrease in faith (*īmān*) is directly proportionate to the increase and decrease of one's love for the Prophet ﷺ, and the good-pleasure of Allah Most High, eternal bliss, and the delights and degrees of the people of Paradise are all in direct proportion to the servant's love for the Prophet ﷺ, just as Allah's displeasure, eternal damnation, and the torment and descending levels of

1 The above-quoted supplication is taken from our Imam al-Shāfiʿī ﷺ. I have taken it from his epistle (*al-Risāla*) narrated by his colleague Imam al-Rabīʿ b. Sulaymān, may Allah have mercy upon him.

Hell for its denizens are all in direct proportion to one's hatred for the Prophet ﷺ.

Another benefit of compiling the Prophet's noble descriptions—for those whom Allah bestows enabling grace—is following him and emulating him in the areas where he can be emulated, such as his largesse, his forbearance, his humility, his renunciation, his worship, and other aspects of his excellent qualities of character and noble states. All of that is cause for Allah's love, which results in eternal bliss in this life and the Next. Allah Most High says, *"Say, 'If you [truly] love Allah, follow me; Allah will love you.'"* (Quran 3:31)

May Allah make us of those who follow the Prophet ﷺ in his upright way and his straight path, and may He resurrect us under his Standard (*liwāʾ*) among his lovers—may salutations and prayers be upon him and all of them!

Chapter One

THE PROPHET'S LINEAGE & NOBLE NAMES ﷺ

SECTION ONE

The Prophet's Lineage 

HE IS OUR master Muḥammad the Messenger of Allah ﷺ, the son of ʿAbdullāh, the son of ʿAbd al-Muṭṭalib[2], the son of Hāshim[3], the son of ʿAbd Manāf[4], the son of Quṣayy[5], the son of Kilāb, the son

2 His actual name was Shayba al-Ḥamd. ʿAbd al-Muṭṭalib was his nickname. It is said that the reason the Prophet's grandfather is called ʿAbd al-Muṭṭalib is because his father Hāshim said (as he was on his deathbed in Mecca) to his brother al-Muṭṭalib, "Go find your servant in Yathrib." It is also said that Shayba's uncle, Muṭṭalib, came with him to Mecca with Shayba riding behind him; and because that is a subservient manner of riding, Muṭṭalib was asked about him, to which he replied, "He is my servant." He was too shy to say that Shayba is his nephew, but once they settled, it became clear that he was. (See, Mullā ʿAlī al-Qārī, *al-Mawrid al-rawī*)

3 His actual name was ʿAmr. He was called Hāshim because when his people suffered drought, he would break (*yahshim*) the bread used for *tharid* (a meat and bread dish). (See, Mullā ʿAlī al-Qārī, *al-Mawrid al-rawī*)

4 His actual name was Mughīra. (See, Mullā ʿAlī al-Qārī, *al-Mawrid al-rawī*)

5 His actual name was Mujammiʿ. The name Quṣayy is a diminutive form of the word *qaṣiyy*, which means remote. He was given this name because he was far away from his family in the lands of Quḍḍāʿa when his mother Fāṭima was pregnant with him. (See, Mullā ʿAlī al-Qārī, *al-Mawrid al-rawī*)

of Murra[6], the son of Kaᶜb, the son of Luᵓayy, the son of Ghālib, the son of Fihr[7], the son of Mālik, the son of Naḍr[8], the son of Kināna, the son of Khuzayma, the son of Mudrika[9], the son of Ilyās, the son of Muḍar, the son of Nizār[10], the son of Maᶜadd, the son of ᶜAdnān.

Up to here there is consensus among the *Umma*; as for the lineage after this up to Ādam, nothing thereof is authentic and reliable. When the Messenger of Allah ﷺ would mention his lineage he would not go past Maᶜadd b. ᶜAdnān b. Udud. He would stop there and say, "The genealogists tell untruths, for Allah says '*And many generations in between*' (Quran 25:38)"[11]

This is the absolute noblest of all genealogies. Al-ᶜAbbās ؓ reported that the Prophet ﷺ said, "Allah created mankind and placed me in their finest group, and then he chose the best of the tribes and placed me the finest tribe, then He chose the best of the households and placed me in the finest household. Thus I am the

6 His actual name was Ḥakīm.

7 His actual name was Quraysh, and it is to him that the tribe of Quraysh traces it lineage.

8 His actual name was Qays.

9 His actual name was ᶜAmr.

10 His actual name was Khaldān. Nizār is derived from the word *nazar*, which means uncommon. He was called Nizār because he was a rarity of his time. Some say that he was called Nizār because when his father looked at him after his birth, he saw the light of the Prophet Muḥammad ﷺ between his eyes and became joyful. As a result of this joy, his father fed many people and said, "This is all *nazar*," i.e., this is all miniscule when it comes to what is owed to this newborn." (See, Mullā ᶜAlī al-Qārī, *al-Mawrid al-rawī*)

11 Ibn Saᶜd, *al-Ṭabaqāt al-kubrā*.

best of them in soul and the best of them in household."[12]

Wāthila b. al-Asqaᶜ ﷺ reported that the Messenger of Allah ﷺ said, "Verily, Allah chose Ismāᶜīl from the sons of Ibrāhīm, and chose Kināna from the sons of Ismāᶜīl, and chose Quraysh from the sons of Kināna, and chose the sons of Hāshim from Quraysh, and chose me from the sons of Hāshim."[13]

Ibn ᶜUmar ﷺ reported that the Messenger of Allah ﷺ said, "Verily Allah appraised His creation and chose from them the sons of Ādam, and from them He chose the Arabs, and from the Arabs He chose Quraysh, and from Quraysh He chose the sons of Hāshim, and from the sons of Hāshim He chose me; and thus I remain the choicest of the choice. Certainly, whosoever loves the Arabs then I love them for they love me; and whosoever hates the Arabs then I hate them for they hate me."[14]

12 Al-Zabīdī, *Itḥāf al-sādat al-muttaqīn*.
13 Al-Tirmidhī, *Sunan*.
14 Al-Ḥākim, *al-Mustadrak*.

SECTION TWO

The Prophet's Noble Names 

KNOW THAT THE Messenger of Allah ﷺ has several names. Imam al-Nawawī said in *Tahdhīb [al-asmāʾ wa al-lughāt]*, "Said the imam and hadith master Qāḍī Abū Bakr Ibn al-ʿArabī al-Mālikī in his work *al-Aḥwadhī*, a commentary upon the *Sunan* of al-Tirmidhī, 'Some of the Sufis have said that Allah—the Exalted and Sublime—has one thousand names, and that the Prophet ﷺ also has one thousand names.'"

Jubayr b. Maṭʿam b. ʿAdī ؓ reported that the Messenger of Allah ﷺ said, "I have several names. I am Muḥammad, I am Aḥmad, I am al-Māḥī (the Obliterator) by whom Allah obliterates disbelief. And I am al-Ḥāshir (the Gatherer) at whose feet humankind shall gather. And I am al-ʿĀqib (the Final) after whom there is no prophet."[15]

Ḥudhayfa ؓ said, "I met the Prophet ﷺ on one of the streets of Medina and he said, 'I am Muḥammad, I am Aḥmad, I am the Prophet of Mercy and the Prophet of Repentance; I am al-Muqaffī, I am al-Ḥāshir (the Gatherer) and the Prophet of *Malāḥim*.'"[16] Al-Muqaffī means the one followed by the Messengers sent before

15 Al-Tirmidhī, *Shamāʾil*.
16 Ibid.

him (and he is the last of them and their Seal). *Malāḥim* means wars (*ḥurūb*), so in being named "the Prophet of Wars" there is an indication that he was sent with fighting and with the sword. No previous prophets and their nations waged jihad as the Prophet Muḥammad ﷺ and his nation did. His nation fought against disbelievers all over the earth and over successive generations, and will continue till they fight against the Anti-Christ (al-Dajjāl).

In *al-Tahdhīb* it says:

> In the Quran, Allah (Exalted and Sublime is He!) called him a Messenger, a Prophet, Trustworthy (Amīn), a witness (Shāhid), a bringer of glad tidings (Mubashir), a warner (Nadhīr), a caller unto Allah with His leave, a shining light (Sirāj Munīr), full of pity (Raʾūf), compassionate (Raḥīm), and one who reminds (Mudhakkir). Allah made him a mercy (Raḥma) and a grace (Niʿma) and a guide (Hādī)—may Allah send prayers and salutations upon him... Ibn ʿAbbās ﷺ reported that the Messenger of Allah ﷺ said, "In the Quran my name is Muḥammad; in the Gospel it is Aḥmad; and in the Torah it is Uḥīd [he who takes to one side]. I was named Uḥīd because I shall keep my nation from the fire of *Jahannam*."

Al-Nawawī added (quoting from the narration of Ibn ʿAsākir), "[I am] al-Fātiḥ (the Opener), Ṭāhā, Yāsīn, ʿAbdullāh, and the Seal of the Prophets."

Al-Qasṭalānī said in *al-Mawāhib*, as did al-Bājūrī in his marginalia on the *Shamāʾil*:

The author of the book *Shawq al-ʿarūs wa uns al-nufūs* (The Bridegroom's Longing and the Souls' Intimacy), Ḥusayn b. Muḥammad al-Dāmaghānī, quoted Kaʿb al-Aḥbār who said, "The name of the Prophet ﷺ among the inhabitants of Paradise is ʿAbd al-Karīm (Servant of the Generous); among the denizens of the Hellfire his name is ʿAbd al-Jabbār (Servant of the Compeller); among the bearers of the Throne (ʿArsh) it is ʿAbd al-Ḥamīd (Servant of the Praised); among the remaining angels it is ʿAbd al-Majīd (Servant of the Glorious); among the Prophets it is ʿAbd al-Wahhāb (Servant of the Bestower); among the devils it is ʿAbd al-Qahhār (Servant of the Overpowering); among the jinn it is ʿAbd al-Raḥīm (Servant of the Compassionate); among the mountains it is ʿAbd al-Khāliq (Servant of the Creator); to the lands it is ʿAbd al-Qādir (Servant of the Omnipotent); to the oceans it is ʿAbd al-Muhaymin (Servant of the Guardian); to the serpents it is ʿAbd al-Quddūs (Servant of the Sanctified); to the insects it is ʿAbd al-Ghiyyāth (Servant of the Provider of Succor); to the wild animals he is ʿAbd al-Razzāq (Servant of the Provider); to the predatory animals he is ʿAbd al-Salām (Servant of the Transcendent Source of Peace); to the domesticated animals he is ʿAbd al-Muʾmin (Servant of the Faithful); and to the fowl he is ʿAbd al-Ghaffār (Servant of the Forgiver). In the Torah he is called Muʾdh-muʾdh; in the Gospel he is called Ṭāb Ṭāb ('He is pure He is pure'); in the tablets he is called ʿĀqib (the Final); in the Psalms he is called Fārūq; with Allah he is called Ṭāhā and Yāsīn; and with the believers he is called

Muḥammad ﷺ. His agnomen is Abū al-Qāsim (distributor) because he distributes Paradise between its inhabitants."

Regarding the name Muʾdh-muʾdh, al-Qasṭalānī quoted al-Suhaylī who said, "I have quoted this from a learned Jewish man who embraced Islam. He said that it means 'the Pure the Pure.'" This name, therefore, has the same meaning as Ṭāb Ṭāb. As for the name Fārūq, it means the one who discerns between truth and falsehood, and it is the meaning of the name Paraclete mentioned in the Gospel of John.

The seal of the hadith masters, Jalāl al-Dīn al-Suyūṭī, wrote an epistle that he called *al-Bahja al-saniyya fī asmāʾ Khayr al-Khalīqa* (The Resplendent Delight on the Names of the Best of Creation). In it he gathered nearly five hundred names. In his *al-Mawāhib*, al-Qasṭalānī quoted the statement of Abū Bakr Ibn al-ʿArabī who said in *Aḥkām al-Qurʾān* that Allah has one thousand names, and that the Prophet ﷺ also has one thousand names. Al-Qasṭalānī commented,

> What is meant here are descriptions (*awṣāf*); all of the names mentioned are descriptions of praise; and if that is the case, then the Prophet ﷺ has one name for every description. Furthermore, some of these names are exclusive to him (or are predominantly used to describe him) while others are shared. All of this is unmistakably clear to all who can see. If we coin a name for each of his descriptions they will reach the number mentioned, or even exceed them... . What I have gathered from the words of our teachers [i.e., al-Ḥāfiẓ al-Sakhāwī] in *al-Qawl al-badīʿ*, as well as Qāḍī ʿIyāḍ in *al-Shifā*, Ibn al-

ʿArabī in *al-Qabas* and *Aḥkām* [al-Qurʾān], and Ibn Sayyid al-Nās and others, is that the [Prophet's] names exceed four hundred...

Al-Qasṭalānī went on to quote all of the names in alphabetical order, and then mentioned the two hundred and one names compiled by Imam al-Jazūlī in *Dalāʾil al-khayrāt*.

Al-Nawawī said in his *Tahdhīb*, "His well-known agnomen is Abū al-Qāsim, and Jibrīl ﷺ called him by the agnomen Abū Ibrāhīm."

"Muḥammad" is the best of the Prophet's names ﷺ. Al-Qasṭalānī said, "This name, as Anas reported in a hadith, was given to him by Allah two thousand years before creation."

Ibn ʿAsākir narrated on the authority of Kaʿb al-Aḥbār who said, "Ādam counselled his son Shīth (Seth), saying, 'Dear son, you are my successor after me so take the position with the fortification of god consciousness and the firmest handhold. Each time you remember Allah, mention the name Muḥammad as well, for I saw that name written upon the arch of the Throne. Thereafter I travelled through the heavens and did not see a single place except that the name Muḥammad was written upon it. My Lord caused me to settle within the Garden and therein I saw neither palace nor lofty room except that the name Muḥammad was written upon it. I saw the name Muḥammad written upon the necks of the heavenly maidens (*al-Ḥūr al-ʿĪn*) and upon the leaves and branches of the trees therein, as well as on the leaves of the Tree of Ṭūbā and the Furthest Lote-tree (*Sidra al-Muntahā*), and upon the curtains of Paradise, between the eyes of the angels—so remember him [Muḥammad] profusely, for verily the angels mention him in all of their moments!'"

Ḥassān b. Thābit ﷺ said:

A seal of Prophethood from Allah has appeared
Upon him, a light, shimmering and witnessed
God attached the name of His Prophet to His name
When the muezzin cries out "I testify" for the five [prayers]
He portioned out to him from His name to exalt him;
For He is the Possessor of the Throne, the one who is praised
And this is Muḥammad [the Oft-praised]!

As for his name Aḥmad, al-Bājūrī said in his gloss (on Imam al-Tirmidhī's *Shamāʾil*):

> It is originally a superlative noun. He was given this name because among those given to praise, he is the most frequent of them in offering praises to his Lord. It is narrated in *Ṣaḥīḥ* [*al-Bukhārī*] that on the Day of Resurrection the Prophet ﷺ shall receive openings of praises that no one else received before. He shall likewise have the Standard of Praise (*Liwāʾ al-Ḥamd*) hoisted for him, and he will be uniquely selected with the Praiseworthy Station (*al-Maqām al-Maḥmūd*).

In short, the Prophet ﷺ has the most praising nature and most praiseworthy nature of all people, and that is why he was named Aḥmad and Muḥammad respectively. These two noble names have a distinction above all other names, so it is a must that extra care be taken with naming [others] with them. It is reported in a sacred hadith tradition (*ḥadīth qudsī*) that Allah said, "I have taken it upon Myself that no one named Aḥmad or Muḥammad shall enter the Hellfire!" And al-Daylamī narrated on the authority of ʿAlī ؓ, "There is no table spread laid out that is attended by someone named Aḥmad or Muḥammad save that Allah will sanctify that house twice each day."

Chapter Two

THE PROPHET'S PHYSICAL DESCRIPTIONS ﷺ

SECTION ONE

The Beauty of the Prophet's Form

AL-QASṬALĀNĪ SAID in *al-Mawāhib,* "Know that it is from the perfection of one's faith in the Prophet ﷺ to believe that Allah Most High created his noble body in a fashion that has not and will not be matched by any other." How excellent is the couplet of al-Būsīrī:

It is he whose meaning and form attained perfection
Then the Maker of Souls chose him as the Beloved
Exalted he is above having a rival in his perfections;
The undivided essence of all beauty

Al-Qurṭubī (may Allah have mercy upon him) said in his *Kitāb al-ṣalāt,* "The Prophet's perfect beauty has not been completely manifested to us, for if it was disclosed to us in full, our eyes would be unable to behold him!"

Several transmitters have narrated that the Messenger of Allah ﷺ had a handsome form.[17] Al-Tirmidhī narrated on the authority of Anas ؓ, "The Messenger of Allah ﷺ was neither excessively tall (*bāʾin*) nor short; he was neither extremely pale (*amhaq*) nor dark brown (*ādam*) in his complexion; and his hair was neither extremely

17 Ibid.

curly (*al-ja*ʿ*d al-qaṭat*) nor lank (*sabṭ*)."[18]

The meaning of *bā*ʾ*in* is one whose tallness is apparent. The meaning of *amhaq* is extreme paleness without any reddishness. The meaning of *ādam* is brown (*asmar*). The meaning of *ja*ʿ*d* is one whose hair is coiled. The meaning of *qaṭaṭ* is one [whose hair] is extremely curly. The meaning of *sabṭ* is one whose hair is straight.

The Messenger of Allah ﷺ had a medium stature, with broad shoulders, and a full head of hair that reached his earlobes[19], with a slight part.[20] His hands and feet were fleshy (*shathn*)[21], his head was large, as were his joints. He had a long, thin line of hair that ran from his chest to his navel. When he walked, he walked as if descending down a slope.[22]

The Messenger of Allah ﷺ had slightly wavy hair with

18 Ibid.

19 In the *Shamā*ʾ*il* works there are three words used to describe the length of the Prophet's hair ﷺ:

Jumma: where the hair reaches down to the shoulders

Wafra: where the hair reaches to the ear lobes

Limma: where the hair reaches between the ear lobes and the shoulders.

20 Ibid.

21 This does not contradict the narration of Anas ؓ who said that he "felt no silk or brocade softer than the palms of the Prophet ﷺ," for they were both soft and thick, demonstrating his immense strength. Imam al-Bājūrī notes that the original meaning of *shathn* is thick and rough, and suggests that the Prophet's hands were soft and delicate but would become rough when needed for jihad and physical labor. It is more likely, however, that the Prophet's weapons and tools softened themselves for his blessed hands rather than his hands becoming rough when handling them. Allah knows best. [t]

22 Al-Tirmidhī, *Shamā*ʾ*il*.

a part. He was not corpulent (*muṭahham*). His face was not completely circular, but was slightly round in shape. His complexion was radiant and mixed [with a bit of redness]. His eyes were very black and his eyelashes were lush. His joints were large and his shoulders were broad. He was not hirsute; a thin line of hair ran from his chest to his navel. His hands and feet were fleshy. When he walked, he walked with vigor, as if he were descending from a slope. When he would turn [to look at someone or something] he would turn with his whole body. Between his shoulders was the Seal of Prophethood—and he ﷺ was the Seal of the Prophets. His heart was the soundest of hearts, his speech was the most truthful of speech, and he was the gentlest of all people in nature and the noblest of them in relations. Whoever saw him unexpectedly would be filled with awe. Whoever came to know him would love him. Whoever would describe him would say, 'I saw neither before him nor after him anyone like him.'"[23]

The cheeks of the Messenger of Allah ﷺ were even[24]. He had a wide mouth, and his chest and abdomen were equal in proportion. He had hair on his shoulders and arms, and on his upper chest. His forearms were long and his palms were wide. He had a slight reddishness in

23 Ibid.

24 That is, his cheeks were not protruding or high on his blessed face ﷺ. [t]

the whites of his eyes,[25] and his tear ducts[26] were red. His heels were not fleshy."[27]

Being described with a wide mouth is a compliment [in Arabic], and it is a sign of eloquence. The Messenger of Allah ﷺ had large eyes and lush eyelashes. [The whites of] his eyes were mixed with slight redness. He ﷺ had a slight, almost indiscernible space between his eyebrows, which appeared as if it was pure silver. His eyes were wide, and his pupils were very dark. Within his eyes there was a slight mixture of redness. His eyelashes were lush, so numerous that they nearly appeared joined.

The Prophet ﷺ had a large head and large hands and feet. He ﷺ had even cheeks that did not protrude. His face was neither elongated nor completely circular.

The Prophet ﷺ was the finest and most beautiful of all people. He was of medium stature, though inclining to tallness. His shoulders were broad and his cheeks were even.[28] His hair was extremely black. The lines of his eyes were dark as if he applied antimony (kohl). His eyelashes were lush. When he would walk he would walk using his entire foot. There was a slight, well-proportioned arch to his feet (*akhmaṣ*).[29] When he would place his shawl over

25 This type of reddishness in the whites of the eyes is considered a sign of prophecy. Al-Ḥāfiẓ al-ʿIrāqī narrates that the monk outside of Bostra, who saw the Prophet ﷺ as a young boy travelling with the trade caravan to Syria, said to Maysara, "In his eyes there is some reddishness—he is the one!" Some of the Gnostics say that the reddishness in the Prophet's eyes ﷺ was because of the intensity of his witnessing of the Divine. [t]

26 The reddish part in the inner corner of the eye from where tears are produced. [t]

27 Al-Tirmidhī, *Shamāʾil.*

28 Ibid.

29 In other words, the Prophet's ﷺ feet had beautiful, well-

his shoulders he would appear like a silver ingot. When he would laugh he would shine.[30]

The Prophet ﷺ had wide forearms, broad shoulders, and lush eyelashes.

His upper arms were well-built, and the bones of his forearm were long. His lower extremities underneath the loincloth were well-built, such as his thighs and shanks. His palms were wide and his extremities long. His fingers were as rods of silver. He was well proportioned and fully fleshed. Towards the end of his days his body became stout, but his flesh was almost as firm as it was in his early years, unharmed by age.[31]

The Prophet ﷺ was the most handsome of people in countenance and the best of them in character. He was neither excessively tall nor short. When walking by himself he would be described as having a medium stature, and never did a tall person walk in his company but that the Messenger of Allah ﷺ was taller than him. At times he would be flanked by two tall men yet he would appear taller than they; and when they would leave him they would be described as tall and he would be described as having medium stature, and he ﷺ would say, "All goodness has been placed in moderation."[32]

Ibn Sabʿ adds in his *Khaṣāʾiṣ* that "When the Prophet ﷺ would sit down, his shoulders would appear higher than the rest of those sitting [with him]."

The Messenger of Allah ﷺ had sublime qualities

proportioned arches. [t]

30 Al-Zabīdī, *Itḥāf al-sādāt al-muttaqīn*. This means that when the Prophet ﷺ would laugh, light could be seen emitting from between his blessed teeth. [t]

31 Al-Ghazālī, *Iḥyāʾ ʿulūm al-dīn*.

32 Abū Bakr b. Lāl, *Makārim al-akhlāq*.

and was honored as such by others. His face shone like the light of the full moon. He was taller than a man of average height, yet shorter than a tall man. His head was large and his hair was wavy. If it parted easily he would part it [in the middle], and if not he would leave it. If he left his hair [without parting it] it would not fall past his earlobes. His complexion was radiant. His forehead was wide. His eyebrows were long and full, perfectly shaped but without connecting. Between them was a vein that would appear when he would become angry. The bridge of his nose was high and light rose from it; the one who did not look closely at him would think that it was large. His beard was thick, his cheeks were even. His mouth was wide and his teeth were well-spaced. He had a thin line of hair that ran from his chest to his navel. His neck was like that of a statue and as resplendent as silver. He was evenly proportioned. He was well-built and fully fleshed, and his chest and stomach were even with each other. His chest and shoulders were broad, and his joints were large. His limbs that were unclothed or without hair shone brightly. Besides the thin line of hair that ran from his chest to his navel, neither his chest nor his stomach had hair. His arms, his shoulders, and his upper chest, however, had hair. He had long forearms and wide and thick palms and feet. His fingers and toes were long and well-proportioned and he had a slight arch in the soles of his feet. His feet were smooth such that water could run right off them [if poured]. When he walked, it was as if he was descending down a slope. When he would turn to look [at someone or something] he would turn with his whole body. He would lower his gaze, and he would look at the ground more than he would look into the sky.

Most of his looking was from the corner of his eye.[33] He would have his Companions walk in front of him and would initiate the greetings of peace with whomever he met.[34]

The Messenger of Allah ﷺ had a slight space between his front teeth; when he would speak, light could be seen emitting from between them.[35]

The Messenger of Allah ﷺ had the most beautiful of all feet.[36]

Maymūna b. Kardam said, "I saw the Messenger of Allah ﷺ and have not forgotten that the length of his big toes exceeded the length of his other toes." (This was narrated by Imam Aḥmad and others.)

The shanks of the Prophet ﷺ had slenderness to them. Slenderness is a praiseworthy quality for shanks.

When the Prophet ﷺ walked, he would walk with vigor, strong of limbs, and without languor. It was as if he was descending from a rock or walking down a slope. He inclined forward as he walked, bringing his footsteps close together without swaggering.[37] When the Messenger of Allah ﷺ would walk, his Companions would walk in front of him and leave his back for the angels.[38]

When the Prophet ﷺ would walk he would not look here or there.[39] When the Prophet ﷺ would walk he

33 That is, he would look casually at people and things and would not stare at them directly. [t]

34 Al-Tirmidhī, *Shamāʾil.*

35 Ibid.

36 Ibn Saʿd, *Ṭabaqāt.*

37 Al-Ghazālī, *Iḥyāʾ ʿulūm al-dīn.*

38 Ibn Mājah, *Sunan.*

39 Al-Ḥākim, *al-Mustadrak.* This means the Prophet ﷺ would

would not look behind him. If at times his shawl would get caught on a tree he would not look over at it until they [his Companions] removed it from him.

When the Prophet ﷺ would walk he would take vigorous strides.[40] He ﷺ would walk in such a way that it was known that he was neither weak nor lazy.[41]

Never would two [or more] men walk directly behind the Prophet ﷺ. If they were three in number he would walk between them, and if they were more he would put some of them to walk in front.[42]

When the Prophet ﷺ would put on his Sandals he would begin with his right foot, and when he would take them off he would begin with his left foot.[43]

When the Prophet ﷺ would enter the mosque he would enter with his right foot. He ﷺ loved using the right hand for everything, taking and giving.

Abū Hurayra ؓ said, "I never saw anyone more beautiful than the Messenger of Allah ﷺ. It was as if the sun shone upon his face. And I never saw anyone who walked faster than the Messenger of Allah ﷺ. It was as if the earth folded itself up for him. We would tire ourselves out in exertion [walking with him] but for him it was effortless."[44]

The Messenger of Allah ﷺ was light. When he would walk in sunlight or moonlight he did not cast a shadow.

---

walk with his eyes focused on the path in front of him and would not busy himself with any distractions on the way. [t]

40 Abū Dāwūd, *Sunan*.

41 Ibn ʿAsākir, *Tārīkh Dimashq*.

42 Al-Shaʿrānī, *Kashf al-ghumma*.

43 Abū Yaʿlā, *Musnad*.

44 Al-Tirmidhī, *Shamāʾil*.

His face was like the sun and the moon and [slightly] circular.

Al-Barāʾ b. ʿĀzib رضي الله عنه said, "I have never seen anyone whose hair reached between his ear lobes and his shoulders dressed in a red garment more handsome than the Messenger of Allah ﷺ.[45]

Abū Hurayra رضي الله عنه said, "I never saw anyone more beautiful than the Messenger of Allah ﷺ. It was as if the sun shone upon his face, and when he would laugh, his light would shine upon the walls..."[46]

Umm Maʿbad رضي الله عنها said in her description of the Prophet ﷺ, "He was the most beautiful of people when seen from afar, and the sweetest and fairest of them when seen up close..."[47]

Jābir b. Samura رضي الله عنه said, "I saw the Messenger of Allah on a full, moonlit night, and he was wearing a red garment. I began to look at him and then look at the moon, and verily he was more beautiful than the moon!"[48]

A man asked al-Barāʾ b. ʿĀzib رضي الله عنه "Was the face of the Messenger of Allah ﷺ like a sword?" Al-Barāʾ replied, "No; rather, it was like the moon."[49]

The Prophet's ﷺ complexion was radiant; he was neither dark brown nor extremely white. His uncle Abū Ṭālib described him thus:

A radiant one, by virtue of whose face the rain is sought
A caretaker of the orphans, a guardian of the widows[50]

45 Ibid.
46 Qāḍī ʿIyāḍ, *al-Shifā*.
47 Aḥmad, *Musnad*.
48 Agreed upon.
49 Al-Bukhārī, *Ṣaḥīḥ*.
50 Ibn Isḥāq, *Sīra*.

The Prophet's ﷺ complexion was radiant, and his sweat ﷺ appeared on his face like beads of pearls. When he would walk he would lean forward.

The Prophet ﷺ was the handsomest and most resplendent of men. No one would describe him without comparing him to the full moon. They [his Companions] used to say that he is as his companion Abū Bakr al-Ṣiddīq ؓ used to describe him:

Honest, the Chosen One, calling unto good
Like the light of the full moon that cleaves darkness[51]

The Prophet ﷺ was radiant, as if fashioned from silver[52], and his hair was wavy.

The Prophet ﷺ was radiant, handsome, and evenly proportioned.

The Prophet's ﷺ complexion was radiant and mixed with reddishness. The pupils of his eyes were dark and his eyelashes were lush.

The Prophet's ﷺ complexion was radiant and mixed with reddishness. His head was large, and his forehead was bright and luminous, and his eyelashes were lush.[53]

The Prophet ﷺ had the most beautiful neck of all of Allah's servants—described as neither long nor short. That part of his neck exposed to the sun or the wind was like a pitcher of silver mixed with gold, shining on account of the radiance of the silver and the redness of the gold.[54] He ﷺ had the most beautiful lips and most

51 Al-Ghazālī, *Iḥyāʾ ʿulūm al-dīn.*
52 Al-Tirmidhī, *Shamāʾil.*
53 Al-Bayhaqī, *Dalāʾil al-Nubuwwa.*
54 Al-Ghazālī, *Iḥyāʾ ʿulūm al-dīn.*

delicate closed mouth of all of Allah's servants.[55] His chest was broad, and his flesh did not overlap; he was like a mirror in its evenness, like the moon in its luminescence. His stomach had three folds: one of them was covered by his loincloth, and the other two were visible.[56]

Umm Hāniʾ ﷺ said, "Whenever I saw the stomach of the Messenger of Allah ﷺ I would be reminded of a folded Egyptian garment."[57]

Muḥarrish al-Kaʿbī ﷺ said, "The Prophet ﷺ set out from Jiʿrāna to perform the ʿUmra; I looked at his back and it looked like pure silver."

In *al-Mawāhib* [*al-laduniyya*] there is a narration from Muqātil b. Ḥayyān, who said, "Allah Most Exalted revealed to ʿĪsā ﷺ: 'Listen and obey, O son of the pure and chaste virgin! I have created you without father and thus made you a sign for all of creation, so worship Me alone, trust in Me alone, and go to your people and tell them that I am Allah, the Living, the Self-sufficient, the Everlasting. Tell them that they must believe in the Primordial Prophet: he of the camel and the armor, of the turban and the Sandals, and of the Staff; he of wavy hair, broad forehead, connected eyebrows, lush eyelashes, dark pupils, aquiline nose, even cheeks, and thick beard; whose beads of sweat glisten on his face like pearls, who emits the scent of musk, and whose neck is like a silver pitcher.'"

Ibn al-Athīr said, "The sound description of the Prophet's eyebrows is that they were long and full but without being fully connected."

When the Messenger of Allah ﷺ would look into

55 Ibid.

56 Ibid.

57 Ibn Hishām, *Sīra*.

a mirror he would say, "All praise is due to Allah who fashioned my creation and gave it even proportion, who honored my face and made it beautiful, and who made me one of the Muslims."[58] [In another narration] when the Messenger of Allah ﷺ would look into a mirror he would say, "All praise is due to Allah who beautified my physical creation and my character, and made sightly my manners while the manners of others are unsightly."[59]

The Prophet ﷺ would say, "I most resemble Ādam ﷺ of all people, and my father Ibrāhīm ﷺ most resembled me in character and in form."[60]

Jābir b. ʿAbdullāh ﷺ reported that the Messenger of Allah ﷺ said, "The Prophets were presented to me, and lo Mūsā resembled one of the men of Shanūʾa.[61] Then I saw ʿĪsā son of Maryam, and the closest person I have seen who bears a resemblance to him is ʿUrwa b. Masʿūd. Then I saw Ibrāhīm, and the closest person I have seen who bears a resemblance to him is this companion of yours.[62] Then I saw Jibrīl, and the closest person I have seen who bears a resemblance to him is Diḥya."[63]

The Messenger of Allah ﷺ had a wide back; between his shoulder blades was the Seal of Prophethood (*Khātam*

58 Ibn al-Sunnī, *ʿAmal al-yawm wa al-layla.*

59 Al-Bayhaqī, *Shuʿab al-īmān*. The meaning of the last phrase, "and made sightly my manners while the manners of others are unsightly," is that Allah adorned the character traits of the Prophet ﷺ and made them beautiful for all to see, and did not make his manners unsightly or bad. [t]

60 Al-Ghazālī, *Iḥyāʾ ʿulūm al-dīn.*

61 Shanūʾa is a tribe from the Yemen whose members are of medium complexion. [t]

62 The Prophet ﷺ is speaking about himself. [t]

63 Muslim, *Ṣaḥīḥ*.

al-Nubuwwa), which was adjacent to his right shoulder: a black mole with a slight yellowish tint with a number of hairs around it that resembled a horse's mane.[64]

The Seal of the Prophet ﷺ was a reddish colored piece of flesh that was like a pigeon's egg [in size].[65] Burayda b. al-Ḥuṣayb ؓ said, "When the Messenger of Allah ﷺ entered Medina[66], Salmān al-Fārisī ؓ came with a tray of fresh dates and they were placed before the Messenger of Allah ﷺ. The Messenger of Allah ﷺ asked, 'Salmān, what is this?' 'It is charity for you and you Companions,' replied Salmān. The Messenger of Allah ﷺ said, 'Remove it, for we do no consume charity.' He [Salmān] removed the tray and returned the next day with the same tray and placed it before the Messenger of Allah ﷺ. The Messenger of Allah ﷺ asked, 'Salmān, what is this?' 'It is a gift for you,' replied Salmān. The Messenger of Allah ﷺ then said to his Companions, 'Come and eat.' Just then, Salmān saw the Seal of Prophethood on the back of the Messenger of Allah ﷺ and immediately believed in him.

"[Salmān] was owned by one of the Jews, but the Messenger of Allah ﷺ purchased his freedom for a certain price in dirhams with the condition that he[67] plant date palm trees for them and tend to them till they produce fruit. So the Messenger of Allah ﷺ planted all of the date palms except for one, which was planted by ʿUmar. All of those date palms [planted by the Messenger of Allah ﷺ] bore fruit that very same year, while the

64 Al-Ghazālī, *Iḥyāʾ ʿulūm al-dīn*.

65 Al-Tirmidhī, *Shamāʾil*.

66 In the first year of the migration. [t]

67 That is, the one who purchased Salmān's freedom—the Messenger of Allah ﷺ. [t]

date palm [planted by ʿUmar] did not bear fruit.[68] The Messenger of Allah ﷺ said, 'What is the matter with this date palm tree?' ʿUmar said, 'O Messenger of Allah, I planted it.' Just then, the Messenger of Allah uprooted the tree and re-planted it, and it bore fruit within the year."[69]

68 This shows the supreme rank of the Prophet ﷺ over others and that even what he plants with his blessed hands surpasses what is planted by others. [t]
69 Al-Tirmidhī, *Shamāʾil*.

SECTION TWO

The Description of the Prophet's Vision & Antimony (Kohl) ﷺ

THE MESSENGER OF Allah ﷺ could see in the darkness of night just as he could see in the brightness of the day.[70] He ﷺ could see who is behind him in the prayer rows just as he could see who was standing in front of him.[71]

The Messenger of Allah ﷺ could see twelve stars in the constellation of the Pleiades.[72]

The Messenger of Allah ﷺ would not sit in a dark house until a lantern was lit for him.[73]

The Messenger of Allah ﷺ liked to look at green growth[74] and moving water.[75] He also liked to look at citron[76] and red apples.[77]

70 Al-Qasṭalānī, *al-Mawāhib al-laduniyya*.

71 Ibid.

72 Ibid.

73 Ibn Saʿd, *Ṭabaqāt*.

74 Pastures, trees, and the like, as indicated by the second phrase "and moving water." [t]

75 Abū Nuʿaym, *al-Ṭibb al-Nabawī*.

76 Ibid.

77 Ibn Qāniʿ, *al-Muʿjam*.

As for the Prophet's ﷺ antimony, when he would use it he would apply it twice in each eye and then once divided between them.[78] What this means is that he would apply it twice in each eye and then divide the last application between both eyes, thereby making it an odd number of times putting kohl on the applicator.

When the Messenger of Allah ﷺ would apply antimony he would apply it an odd number of times, and when he would burn [incense][79] he would light it an odd number of times.[80]

The Messenger of Allah ﷺ had an antimony container from which he would apply antimony each night, thrice in his right eye and thrice in his left.[81]

Whether resident or travelling, the Messenger of Allah ﷺ was never without five things: a mirror, an antimony container, a comb, a tooth-stick, and a pick (*midrā*).[82] A *midrā* is made from either metal or wood. It is in the shape of the tooth of a comb, though it could be longer. It picks out knotted hair and is used by one who does not have a comb.

Ibn ʿAbbās ﷺ reported that the Prophet ﷺ said, "Apply *ithmid*, for it strengthens the eyesight and boosts the growth of the eyelashes."[83] Al-Bājūrī said, "This is addressed to those with healthy eyesight. As for those suffering from eye ailments, the use of *ithmid* is harmful.

78 Al-Ṭabarānī, *al-Muʿjam al-kabīr*.

79 This is the interpretation of Shaykh Muḥammad b. Sālim al-Ḥifnī and Shaykh ʿAbd al-Raʾūf al-Munāwī in their respective commentaries. [t]

80 Aḥmad, *Musnad*.

81 Al-Tirmidhī, *Shamāʾil*.

82 Al-ʿUqaylī, *al-Ḍuʿafāʾ*.

83 Al-Tirmidhī, *Shamāʾil*.

Ithmid is the well-known mineral used as an antimony. Its mines are found in the east, and its color is a reddish black." Al-Bājūrī also said, after citing the phrase "it strengthens the eyesight": "This is if it is applied by someone who is accustomed to it. If someone who is not accustomed to it applies it, his eyes will become inflamed."

SECTION THREE

The Description of the Prophet's Hair, His Gray Hairs, His Dye, & Related Matters ﷺ

THE MESSENGER OF Allah ﷺ had beautiful wavy hair that was neither excessively curly nor lank. When he combed his hair it appeared as streaks of sand. He would occasionally plait his hair into four braids; each ear would come out between the two braids [on each side]. At other times, he would put his hair over his ears and the locks of hair on his temples would shine.[84]

The hair of the Messenger of Allah ﷺ was less than *jumma* and more than *wafra*.[85]

The Prophet's hair ﷺ reached his shoulders, and would often reach his ear lobes.[86]

The Messenger of Allah ﷺ had a perfectly proportioned body. He was broad shouldered and had hair reaching his shoulders. At times his hair reached his ear

84 Al-Ghazālī, *Iḥyāʾ ʿulūm al-dīn*.
85 Abū Dāwūd, *Sunan*. *Jumma* describes hair when it reaches to the shoulders, and *wafra* describes hair when it reaches to the ear lobes. This narration means that the Prophet's hair ﷺ reached between his ear lobes and his shoulders (also called *limma*). [t]
86 Al-Shaʿrānī, *Kashf al-ghumma*.

lobes, and at other times it reached the mid-point of his ears.[87]

The Messenger of Allah ﷺ would let his hair fall [without parting it]. The idol-worshippers used n, .mto part their hair, and the People of the Scripture (Ahl al-Kitāb) let their hair hang, and the Messenger of Allah ﷺ preferred to accord with the practices of the People of the Scripture so long as he was not given a specific command regarding the matter. Thereafter the Messenger of Allah ﷺ started to part his hair.[88]

The Messenger of Allah ﷺ had a handsome *sabala*.[89] The *sabala* is the front part of the beard that descends toward the chest. The Messenger of Allah ﷺ had a thick beard, which he would let grow while clipping from his moustache.[90]

The Messenger of Allah ﷺ would trim from the length and width of his noble beard.[91]

The Messenger of Allah ﷺ would comb his beard frequently.[92]

The Prophet's tooth-stick and comb would never leave his side ﷺ, and when he would comb his beard he would look into a mirror.[93]

When the Messenger of Allah ﷺ was in a state of concern about something he would rub his beard.[94]

87 Al-Nawawī, *Tahdhīb al-asmāʾ wa al-lughāt*.
88 Al-Tirmidhī, *Shamāʾil*.
89 Al-Ṭabarānī, *al-Muʿjam al-kabīr*.
90 Al-Ghazālī, *Iḥyāʾ ʿulūm al-dīn*.
91 Al-Tirmidhī, *al-Jāmiʿ*.
92 Al-Munāwī, *Kunūz al-ḥaqāʾiq*.
93 Al-Ṭabarānī, *al-Muʿjam al-awsaṭ*.
94 Abū Nuʿaym, *al-Ṭibb al-Nabawī*.

When he felt sadness he would grasp his beard with his hand and look at it.[95]

When the Messenger of Allah ﷺ performed ablutions he would run his fingers through his beard with water.[96]

The Messenger of Allah ﷺ would frequently apply oil to his head and comb his beard, and would often use a *qināʿ*.[97] A *qināʿ* is a piece of cloth placed on top of the head when oil is used, protecting the turban and cloths [from the oil]. When the Messenger of Allah ﷺ would apply oil he would pour it into the palm of his left hand.[98] He would start with his eyebrows and then his eyes and then his head.[99]

The Messenger of Allah ﷺ liked to start from the right side when he would wash himself, part his hair, wear sandals, and in all of his affairs.[100] He would use his left hand when cleaning himself after using the lavatory and when removing spit, phlegm, and the like.[101]

When the Messenger of Allah ﷺ would lie down, he would lie down on his right side, facing the *qibla*.[102] He would use his right hand for eating, drinking, making ablutions, dressing, giving, and taking, and he would use his left hand for everything else.[103]

95 Al-Shīrāzī, *al-Alqāb*.
96 Al-Suyūṭī, *al-Jāmiʿ al-ṣaghīr*.
97 Al-Tirmidhī, *Shamāʾil*.
98 That is, he would pour it into his left hand and then take it and apply it with his right hand. [t]
99 Al-Shīrāzī, *al-Alqāb*.
100 Aḥmad, *Musnad*.
101 Abū Dāwūd, *Sunan*.
102 Al-Nawawī, *Tahdhīb al-asmāʾ wa al-lughāt*.
103 Aḥmad, *Musnad*.

ʿĀʾisha said, "I would comb out the hair of the Messenger of Allah while menstruating."[104]

The Messenger of Allah would comb his hair one day and leave it the next.[105]

The gray hairs on the head and beard of the Messenger of Allah were few in number, around seventeen hairs in total. Abū Bakr said, "O Messenger of Allah, you have some gray hairs!" The Messenger of Allah responded, "Hūd, Wāqiʿa, Mursalāt, ʿAmma yatasāʾalūn, and Idhā al-shamsu kuwwirat[106] have turned my hair gray!"[107] (That was because these Chapters detail the states that will be experienced on the Day of Resurrection, which caused the Prophet to fear for his nation.)

Abū Hurayra was asked, "Did the Messenger of Allah dye his hair?" He replied, "Yes."[108] ʿAbdullāh b. Muḥammad b. ʿAqīl said, "I saw the hair of the Messenger of Allah with Anas, and it was dyed."[109] In the rigorously authenticated collections of al-Bukhārī and Muslim there are reports with multiple routes of transmission that say the Prophet did *not* dye his hair, as his gray hairs did not reach that point. Rather, his strands of hair that were in the possession of others were dyed after his passing so that they would last longer.

In the rigorously authentic collections of al-Bukhārī and Muslim, as well as the *Sunan* of Abū Dāwūd, there is

104 Al-Tirmidhī, *Shamāʾil*.
105 Ibid.
106 Chapters 11, 56, 77, 78, and 81 of the Quran. [t]
107 Ibid.
108 Al-Tirmidhī, *Shamāʾil*.
109 Ibid.

a report from Ibn ʿUmar ﷺ who said that the Messenger of Allah dyed his beard yellow with mallotus (*wars*)[110] and saffron. Qatāda said, "I asked Anas b. Mālik, 'Did the Messenger of Allah ﷺ dye his hair?' He replied, 'They did not reach that point; he had but a few gray hairs on his temples. Abū Bakr, however, did dye his hair with henna and *katam*.'"[111] *Katam* is a reddish colored plant.

Al-Nawawī said, "The preferred opinion is that the Prophet ﷺ dyed his hair on occasion and did not dye is most of the time, thus every [narrator] relayed what he saw and was truthful in his account."

The Messenger of Allah ﷺ commanded others to change the color of their hair in order to be different from the non-Arabs.

The Messenger of Allah would use *nūra*[112] each month and pair his nails every fifteen days.[113] When the Messenger of Allah ﷺ would use *nūra* he would apply it to his pubic area himself.[114] When he would apply *nūra* to his body, he would start with his private areas [himself] and one of his wives would apply it to the other areas of his body.[115]

The Messenger of Allah ﷺ would pair his nails and clip his mustache on Fridays before leaving for the prayer.[116]

110 A plant from the Kamala tree from which a yellowish dye is produced. [t]

111 Al-Tirmidhī, *Shamāʾil*.

112 *Nūra* is a lime depilatory (used for hair removal). [t]

113 Ibn ʿAsākir, *Tārīkh Dimashq*.

114 Ibn Saʿd, *Ṭabaqāt*.

115 Ibn Mājah, *Sunan*.

116 Al-Bayhaqī, *Shuʿab al-īmān*.

The Messenger of Allah ﷺ ordered that clipped hair and nails be buried.[117] He ordered that seven things of a person should be buried: clipped hair, nails, blood, menstrual cloths, teeth, the umbilical cord, and the placenta.[118]

Anas ﷺ said, "I saw the Messenger of Allah as the barber was cutting his hair. His Companions were circling around him and did not want but that one of his hairs fall into their hand."[119]

117 Al-Ṭabarānī, *al-Muʿjam al-kabīr*.
118 Al-Ḥakīm al-Tirmidhī, *Nawādir al-uṣūl*.
119 Muslim, *Ṣaḥīḥ*.

SECTION FOUR

The Description of the Prophet's Sweat & His Natural Scent ﷺ

MUSLIM NARRATED FROM Anas ﷺ who said, "The Messenger of Allah ﷺ would perspire much."[120] His sweat ﷺ appeared on his face like beads of pearls, and it was finer in scent than the strongest musk.[121] When revelation descended upon the Prophet ﷺ it would weigh heavily upon him, and sweat would appear on his brow like beads of pearls—even during a cold day.[122]

The Prophet ﷺ would go to the home of Umm Sulaym and take a midday nap there, and she would spread out for him a mat to sleep on. He would perspire much, so Umm Sulaym soaked up his sweat and put it inside [her] perfume. Upon waking, the Prophet ﷺ asked her, "What are you doing, Umm Sulaym?" She said, "We use your sweat as perfume, and it is the finest of scents!" And in another narration, Umm Sulaym said, "O Messenger of Allah! We seek its blessings for our young children." The Prophet ﷺ said to her, "You are correct."[123]

The palms of the Prophet's hands ﷺ were softer than

120 Muslim, *Ṣaḥīḥ*.
121 Al-Zabīdī, *Itḥāf al-sādāt al-muttaqīn*.
122 Al-Muttaqī al-Hindī, *Kanz al-ʿummāl*.
123 Al-Bayhaqī, *al-Sunan al-kubrā*.

silk, and his scent was like that of the hand of a perfumer, whether he applied scent or not. When he would shake someone's hand, that person would smell the Prophet's scent upon him for the remainder of his day. And when the Prophet ﷺ would pat the head of a young child, that young child would stand out among all other children due to the scent of his head.

Anas ؓ said, "I have touched neither silk nor brocade softer than the palms of Allah's Messenger ﷺ."[124]

Jābir b. Samura ؓ reported that the Messenger of Allah ﷺ touched his cheek. He said, "I experienced a coolness and fragrance from his hand; his hand smelled like he took it out of a perfumist's container."[125]

When the Prophet ﷺ would make his way somewhere, his presence would be known from the wafts of fine scent. Whenever a person walked down a path after the Prophet ﷺ had walked down it, he would know from the fine smell of his sweat that he was there. Isḥāq b. Rāhawayh remarked about this, "That was his natural smell without perfume."

It is reported by Umm ʿĀṣim, the wife of ʿUtba b. Farqad al-Sulamī, "I was one of ʿUtba's four wives, and there was not a single wife among us that did not work hard to ensure that she smelled better than the others. ʿUtba did not apply scent unless it was oil that he put in his beard, and yet despite that he smelled better than all of us, and when he would go out people would say, 'We have never smelled a fragrance finer than ʿUtba's!' So I said to him one day, 'We work hard to wear fine perfume, yet you smell more fragrant than all of us. How

124 Ibn ʿAdī, *al-Kāmil fi al-ḍuʿafāʾ*.
125 Ibn Saʿd, *Ṭabaqāt*.

can that be?' He said, 'I suffered a skin condition during the time of Allah's Messenger ﷺ and I went to him and complained about it. He ordered me to undress, so I did, and I sat before him covering my private parts with my garments. He then blew spittle into his hand and rubbed my back and stomach with it. Since that day, this fragrance has remained with me.'"[126]

Abū Yaʿlā and al-Ṭabarānī both narrated the story of the poor man who sought the Prophet's help ﷺ in preparing his daughter for marriage. The Prophet called for a vessel and rubbed some of his sweat therein, then he said, "Instruct her to use this as perfume." When she put it on, everyone in Medina could smell it, and so they named the family "The House of the Fragrant Ones."

126 Al-Ṭabarānī, *al-Muʿjam al-ṣaghīr*.

SECTION FIVE

The Description of the Prophet's Perfume & His Application Thereof

ANAS B. MĀLIK ‎ﷺ reported, "The Messenger of Allah ﷺ had *sukka* perfume which he would apply on himself." *Sukka* is a mixture of several perfumes. It could also refer to a vessel.[127]

The Messenger of Allah ﷺ would take musk and rub it on his head and beard.[128] The Messenger of Allah ﷺ would [also] anoint his head with musk.

Anas would never refuse to accept a perfume. He said, "The Prophet ﷺ never refused perfume."[129]

Abū ʿUthmān al-Nahdī reported, "The Messenger of Allah ﷺ said, 'When one of you is given an aromatic plant (*rayḥān*) do not refuse it, for it has come from Paradise.'"[130] Anas said, "The most beloved of aromatic plants to the Prophet ﷺ was the henna flower."[131]

The Messenger of Allah ﷺ liked pleasant smells. He ﷺ loved fine scent and pleasant fragrances and

127 Al-Tirmidhī, *al-Shamāʾil*.
128 Al-Muttaqī al-Hindī, *Kanz al-ʿummāl*.
129 Al-Tirmidhī, *al-Shamāʾil*.
130 Ibid.
131 Al-Muttaqī al-Hindī, *Kanz al-ʿummāl*.

would use them frequently and encourage their use, saying, "Three things of your world have been made beloved to me: women, perfume, and the coolness of my eyes has been placed in the prayer."[132] The narration "Three things of your world have been made beloved to me..." is without basis, as [al-Qasṭalānī] has stated in *al-Mawāhib*:

> Shaykh al-Islām al-Ḥāfiẓ Ibn Ḥajar has said,
>
> "The phrase 'three things...' has not appeared in any of the transmission routes for this hadith, and its addition spoils the meaning. This was likewise stated by al-Walī al-ʿIrāqī in his *Amālī*, and in his words, 'This phrase "three things..." is not found in any of the books of hadith, and indeed it spoils the meaning, because prayer is not from the things of this world.' This was also stated explicitly by al-Zarkashī and others, and mentioned approvingly by our teacher [al-Ḥāfiẓ al-Sakhāwī] in *al-Maqāṣid al-ḥasana*."

This addition was also disapproved by Ibn al-Qayyim.

The Messenger of Allah ﷺ loved fine scent and disliked foul odors.[133]

132 Al-Nasāʾī, *al-Sunan*.
133 Al-Bayhaqī, *al-Sunan al-kubrā*.

SECTION SIX

The Description of the Prophet's Voice ﷺ

ANAS ﵁ SAID, "Allah never sent a Prophet save with a beautiful face and a beautiful voice, and your Prophet was the most beautiful of them in face and voice. The voice of Allah's Messenger ﷺ could carry where other voices could not.[134] Al-Barāʾ ﵁ said, "The Messenger of Allah ﷺ addressed us with such a voice that he caused the maidens[135] to hear him in their chambers."[136]

ʿĀʾisha ﵂ said, "The Messenger of Allah ﷺ sat on the pulpit one Friday and said to the people, 'Sit down,' and ʿAbdullāh b. Rawāḥa ﵁, who was all the way in Banī Ghanm[137], heard him and sat down where he was."

ʿAbd al-Raḥmān b. Muʿādh al-Tamīmī ﵁ said, "The Prophet addressed us at Mina, and Allah opened

134 Al-ʿAsqalānī, *Fatḥ al-Bārī*.
135 "Maidens" here means young girls who have just reached puberty. It is said that is also means a girl who has yet to leave her parents, and yet to get married, although she has reached the age of maturity and youth. Jābir mentioned the maidens in particular because of their distance and their being secluded in their homes. Their hearing the Prophet's voice is a sign of the strength of his voice and its reaching where other voices could not.
136 Aḥmad, *Musnad*.
137 Banī Ghanm was a branch from the tribe of Khazraj. [t]

up our faculties of hearing to the extent that we could hear what the Prophet was saying even while we were in our dwellings."[138]

It is related that Umm Hānīʾ ﷺ said, "We could hear the Prophet ﷺ reciting [the Quran] in the middle of the night in the Kaʿba while I was in my bed!"[139]

When the Messenger of Allah ﷺ would deliver sermons, his anger would intensify, and his voice would raise as though he were warning an army, saying, "Your enemy is approaching, morning and evening!"

138 Abū Dāwūd, *Sunan*.
139 Al-Bayhaqī, *Dalāʾil al-Nubuwwa*.

SECTION SEVEN

The Description of the Prophet's Anger ﷺ

BECAUSE OF THE purity of his skin, when the Messenger of Allah would become angry, his pleasure and anger were discernable from his face. When the Messenger of Allah ﷺ would become angry, his cheeks would turn red[140]; if he became angry whilst standing, he would sit down, and if he became angry whilst sitting, he would lie down and his anger would dissipate.[141] If he ﷺ became angry, no one dared approach him, except for ʿAlī ﷺ.[142] [That said,] the Prophet ﷺ was the furthest of people from anger, and the swiftest of them to satisfaction.

The Prophet ﷺ would become angry for the sake of his Lord (Exalted and Sublime is He!), and would not become angry for his own sake.[143] He would do what was right even if it resulted in harm for himself or his Companions, and when he disliked a thing, his dislike of it could be discerned from his face.[144]

140 Al-Ṭabarānī, *al-Muʿjam al-kabīr*.
141 Al-Zabīdī, *Itḥāf al-sādāt al-muttaqīn*.
142 Al-Muttaqī al-Hindī, *Kanz al-ʿummāl*.
143 Ibid.
144 Aḥmad, *Musnad*.

As for the happiness of Allah's Messenger ﷺ, whenever the Prophet ﷺ felt happy, his face lit up as though it were the full moon.[145] And when he was happy ﷺ, it was as though his face were a mirror, and as though the reflection from the walls could be seen upon it.

145 Al-Bukhārī, *Ṣaḥīḥ*.

SECTION EIGHT

The Description of the Prophet's Laughter, Weeping, & Sneezing ﷺ

WHEN THE MESSENGER of Allah ﷺ would laugh, it was mostly smiles, and it would appear as though light were emitting from his teeth, revealing something like hailstones.[146]

Most of the Prophet's laughter ﷺ was in the form of smiles. ʿAbdullāh b. al-Ḥārith ؓ said, "I never saw anyone who smiled as much as the Messenger of Allah ﷺ."[147]

It is related that ʿĀʾisha ؓ said, "I never saw the Messenger of Allah ﷺ bellowing in laughter; however, when he laughed I could see his uvula."[148]

ʿAbdullāh b. al-Ḥārith also said, "The laughter of Allah's Messenger ﷺ was nothing but a smile."[149]

The Messenger of Allah ﷺ would not converse except that he would smile while doing so. The laughter of his Companions, while in his presence ﷺ, would consist of smiles without sound—and that was out of emulation of and respect for him ﷺ. When they would sit in his

146 Al-Tirmidhī, *al-Jamiʿ*.
147 Al-Tirmidhī, *Shamāʾil*.
148 Al-Ḥākim, *al-Mustadrak*.
149 Al-Tirmidhī, *al-Jamiʿ*.

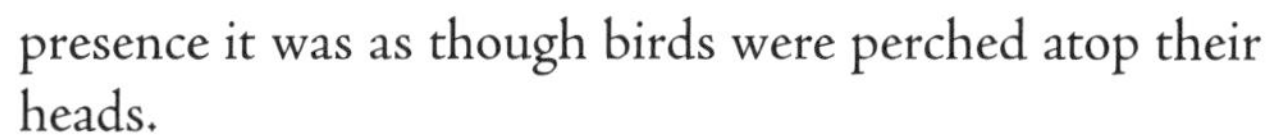

presence it was as though birds were perched atop their heads.

When the Prophet ﷺ would be taken in laughter, he would cover his hand over his mouth.[150]

There are hadith narrations that speak of the Prophet ﷺ laughing till his molar teeth were visible, although most of the time he would be smiling. It is related from Abū Dharr ؓ, "The Messenger of Allah ﷺ said, 'I know the first man to enter Paradise, and the first man to exit Hell. A man will be brought forward on the Day of Resurrection and it will be said, "Present his minor sins to him"—his major sins will be hidden from him. It will then be said to him, "You did such-and-such [sin] on this day..." He will acknowledge each of them and will not deny them, and he will be fearful over his major sins. Then it will be said, "Give him a good deed in place of every sin he committed," and he will say, "I have many sins which I do not see here!"' I [Abū Dharr] then saw the Messenger of Allah ﷺ laugh so much that his molars became visible."[151]

It is related that ʿAbdullāh b. Masʿūd ؓ said, "The Messenger of Allah ﷺ said, 'I know the last man to exit Hell. It will be a man who will exit crawling, and it will be said to him, "Go forth and enter Paradise!" He will make his way to enter, and will find that people have already taken up residence in the dwellings therein, so he will return to where he was before and say, "O Lord! The people have all taken up residence in the dwellings therein!" Then it will be said to him, "Do you remember the time you were in [in the lower world]?" He will reply, "Yes," and then he will be told, "Wish." He will wish, and

150 Al-Muttaqī al-Hindī, *Kanz al-ʿummāl.*
151 Al-Tirmidhī, *Shamāʾil.*

it will be said to him, "For you is all that you have wished for, ten times the world." The man will say, "Do you make fun of me even though you are the Sovereign King?'" I [ᶜAbdullāh b. Masᶜūd] then saw the Messenger of Allah ﷺ laugh until his molars became visible."[152]

ᶜĀmir b. Saᶜd b. Abī Waqqās related, "Saᶜd [his father] ﷺ said, 'I saw the Prophet ﷺ laugh during the Battle the Trench [al-Khandaq] to such an extent that his molar teeth were visible.' I asked, 'What caused him to laugh?' He replied, 'Saᶜd was an archer, and there was a man [among the disbelievers] with a shield who was moving it from side to side in order to protect his forehead. Saᶜd removed an arrow from his quiver and placed it in the bow, and when the man raised his head Saᶜd fired the arrow at him and did not miss the mark [he struck him on the forehead]. The man fell to the ground and his feet were raised upwards. The Prophet ﷺ laughed until his molar teeth were visible.' I asked, 'What caused him to laugh?' He replied, 'The action of Saᶜd with that man.'"[153]

ᶜAlī b. Rabīᶜa said, "I witnessed ᶜAlī as an mount was brought for him to ride. When he placed his foot in the stirrup he said '[I mount] in the name of Allah.' Then, when he hoisted himself up and took a seat on its back, he said 'All praise is due to Allah,' then he recited the verse '*Glorified is He who has subjected this to us; and we could not otherwise subdue it. Certainly, to our Lord we shall return.*' (Quran 43:13–14) Then he said 'All praise is due to Allah' three times, and 'Allah is the Greatest'

152 Ibid.

153 The reason why ᶜĀmir asked his father twice was because he was unsure if the Prophet ﷺ had laughed at the action of Saᶜd striking his target, or had laughed because of the man falling back with his feet upwards and nakedness exposed. [t]

three times, and, 'Glorified and exalted are You, certainly I have wronged my soul, so please forgive me, for none forgives sins except You'—then he laughed. I asked, 'What caused you to laugh, O Leader of the Believers?' He replied, 'I saw the Messenger of Allah ﷺ do just as I did and then laugh. I asked him, "What caused you to laugh, O Messenger of Allah?" and he replied, "Verily your Lord is amazed [pleased] with His servant when he says 'O Lord, forgive me of my sins,' knowing that there is none besides Him who can forgive sins."'"[154]

As for the weeping of the Messenger of Allah ﷺ, it was similar in nature to his laughter: it was neither loud sobbing nor with a raised voice, just as his laughter was not boisterous. Rather, when he would weep, his eyes would shed tears that would flow down [upon his cheeks], and a sound like that of a [boiling] kettle could be heard from his chest. His weeping was either out of mercy for someone who had died, or out of fear and worry for his nation, or out of reverential awe for Allah Most High, or when hearing the Quran, and sometimes when praying the night vigil prayer.

ʿAbdullāh b. al-Shikkhīr ؓ said, "I once went to the Messenger of Allah ﷺ as he was praying, and a sound like that of a [boiling] kettle could be heard from his chest due to his weeping."[155]

ʿAbdullāh b. Masʿūd ؓ reported, "The Messenger of Allah ﷺ said to me, 'Recite [the Quran] to me.' I said, 'O Messenger of Allah! Shall I recite to you when it is you to whom it was revealed?' He replied, 'I love to hear it from

154 Al-Tirmidhī, *Shamāʾil*.
155 Ibid.

others.' So I recited from the Chapter of al-Nisāʾ till I reached the verse '...*and We bring you as a witness over all of these,*' and then I saw that the eyes of the Messenger of Allah ﷺ were flowing with tears."[156]

Ibn ʿAbbās said, "The Messenger of Allah ﷺ picked up his young granddaughter[157] as she was nearing death. He held her in his arms and then put her down in front of himself, where she died.[158] Umm Ayman cried loudly, whereupon the Prophet ﷺ asked her, 'Do you cry in the presence of the Messenger of Allah?'[159] She replied, 'Have I not seen you cry?' He replied, 'I do not cry [like that]; rather, it is a mercy. The believer enjoys a good state at all times, and even when his soul is removed from his body he praises Allah, Exalted and Sublime is He!'"[160]

Anas b. Mālik said, "We witnessed the burial of the daughter[161] of the Messenger of Allah ﷺ, and the Messenger of Allah ﷺ was sitting at the head of the grave. I saw his eyes flowing with tears."[162]

ʿĀʾisha reported that the Messenger of Allah ﷺ kissed ʿUthmān b. Maẓʿūn, who had died, while weeping. ʿUthmān b. Maẓʿūn was his brother via nursing.

The Prophet ﷺ would shed tears frequently. On one occasion the sun was eclipsed, and the Prophet began to

156 Ibid.

157 She was Umāma, the daughter of the Prophet's daughter Zaynab. [t]

158 The meaning of the phrase "where she died" means "where she neared death": Umāma survived and later married Imam ʿAlī b. Abī Ṭālib. [t]

159 This means, "Do you cry in a prohibited manner, accompanied by wailing that indicates extreme anguish?"

160 Al-Tirmidhī, *Shamāʾil.*

161 Umm Kulthūm. [t]

162 Al-Tirmidhī, *Shamāʾil.*

cry whilst in prayer, weeping as he supplicated, "O Lord! Have you not promised me that You will not punish them while I am in their midst, and while they seek your forgiveness, and we seek Your forgiveness, O Lord?"[163]

As for the sneezing of the Messenger of Allah ﷺ: When he would sneeze he would place his hand or the corner of his garment over his mouth in order to suppress its sound.[164] When he would sneeze, the Prophet ﷺ would praise Allah, and then it would be said to him "May Allah have mercy upon you," to which he would reply, "May Allah guide you and set right your affair."[165] The Prophet ﷺ disliked loud sneezing inside of the mosque[166], and disliked that one raise his voice when doing it.[167]

As for yawning, the Prophet ﷺ disliked it from others[168]—and Allah Most High had protected him from it, and indeed no Prophet ever yawned.

163 Ibid.
164 Abū Dāwūd, *Sunan*.
165 Aḥmad, *Musnad*.
166 Al-Bayhaqī, *al-Sunan al-kubrā*.
167 Al-Suyūṭī, *al-Durr al-manthūr*.
168 Al-Tirmidhī, *Shamāʾil*.

SECTION NINE

The Description of the Prophet's Speech ﷺ

ʿĀʾISHA REPORTED, "The Messenger of Allah would not draw out his speech as you all do; he would speak clearly and lucidly and would space out his words. Anyone who sat with him would remember what he had said."[169]

The Prophet's speech was in a smooth, measured pitch[170], and all who heard him speak could remember what he said.[171] When the Prophet ﷺ would speak, he would repeat his words three times so he would be understood, and when he would go to a group of people he would greet them three times.[172] When he would sit down to converse with someone, he would often raise his eyes up to the sky.[173] His speech was such that if someone wanted to count his words he would be able to do so.[174]

The Prophet ﷺ would remain silent for long periods of

169 Al-Tirmidhī, *Shamāʾil*.
170 Abū Dāwūd, *Sunan*.
171 Al-Muttaqī al-Hindī, *Kanz al-ʿummāl*.
172 Al-Tirmidhī, *Shamāʾil*.
173 Abū Dāwūd, *Sunan*.
174 Muslim, *Ṣaḥīḥ*.

time.[175] He would keep quiet for long periods and would not speak without need. He would turn away from those who spoke rudely.[176] He would hold his tongue from speaking on any matter save what concerned him.[177]

The Prophet ﷺ was of few words; he was gentle in speech, and would repeat his words twice so he would be understood. The Prophet's speech was like stringed pearls. He ﷺ would turn away from all foul speech, and when forced to mention things that are normally considered filthy, he would refer to them with euphemisms. The Prophet ﷺ would remember Allah between each footstep he would take.[178]

175 Al-Bayhaqī, *al-Sunan al-kubrā*.
176 Al-Tirmidhī, *Shamāʾil*.
177 Al-Baghawī, *Sharḥ al-Sunna*.
178 Al-Muttaqī al-Hindī, *Kanz al-ʿummāl*.

SECTION TEN

The Description of the Prophet's Strength ﷺ

THE MESSENGER OF Allah ﷺ was extremely powerful.[179] Ibn Isḥāq and others relate that there was a man in Mecca who was very strong and skilled in wrestling. People from all over would come to challenge him and he would defeat them all. One day, as this man was in one of the mountain ravines of Mecca, he encountered the Messenger of Allah ﷺ, who said to him, "O Rukāna! Why do you not fear Allah and accept that to which I invite you?" Rukāna said, "Muḥammad, is there a corroborating proof that will show that you are truthful?" The Prophet ﷺ said, "What if I throw you down—will you believe in Allah and His Messenger?" Rukāna replied, "I will, Muḥammad!" The Prophet ﷺ said to him, "Ready yourself for a wrestling match." Rukāna then said, "I am ready." Then the Messenger of Allah came near to Rukāna, grabbed him, and threw him to the ground. Shocked, Rukāna asked the Prophet to absolve him of his agreement [to believe in Allah and His Messenger if defeated] and asked for a rematch. They had a second and a third rematch, and he was thrown down each time.

179 Al-Zabīdī, *Itḥāf al-sādāt al-muttaqīn*.

After the third defeat, Rukāna stood up and said, "You are amazing!"[180]

The Prophet ﷺ wrestled others besides Rukāna, such as Abū al-Aswad al-Jumaḥī, who was so strong that he could stand on a cow hide and ten men would try to pull the hide from under his feet, but it would be torn to bits without him moving one inch. The Prophet ﷺ challenged him to a wrestling match and Abū al-Aswad said, "If you defeat me, I will believe in you." But when the Messenger of Allah wrestled him and defeated him he did not profess faith.

As for the Prophet's sexual strength and stamina, Anas ؓ said, "The Prophet ﷺ would, in the span of a few hours in the night and day, visit each of his eleven wives [and have intimate relations with each of them]."[181]

Ibn Manīᶜ narrated that the Messenger of Allah ﷺ would visit each of nine wives in the forenoon [and have intimate relations with each of them]."[182]

A raised (*marfūᶜ*) report is related on the authority of Ṣafwān b. Sulaym, that the Prophet ﷺ said, "The Angel Jibrīl ؑ came to me with a pot from which I ate, and I was then granted the sexual stamina of forty men combined."[183]

It is related on the authority of Ṭāwūs and Mujāhid that the Prophet ﷺ was given the sexual stamina of forty men combined.

And in another narration from Mujāhid, "He was given the sexual stamina of forty or so men from the people of Paradise."

180 Ibn Kathīr, *al-Bidāya wa al-nihāya*.
181 Aḥmad, *Musnad*.
182 Ibid.
183 Al-Muttaqī al-Hindī, *Kanz al-ᶜummāl*.

It is related in a raised report from Zayd b. Arqam that the Prophet ﷺ said, "A man from the people of Paradise shall be given the appetite of one hundred men in eating, drinking, intimate relations, and sexual desire."[184]

184 Al-Dārimī, *Sunan*.

Chapter Three

THE DESCRIPTION OF THE PROPHET'S CLOTHING, BEDDING, & WEAPONRY 

SECTION ONE

The Description of the Prophet's Clothing: His Shirt, Loin cloth, Shawl, Cap, & Turban ﷺ

Qāḍī ʿIyāḍ (may Allah have mercy upon him) said in *al-Shifā*:

> Examine the biography of our Prophet ﷺ and his character in dealing with wealth. You will find that he was given the treasures of the earth and the keys to the lands. Spoils, which had not been lawful for any Prophet before him, were allowed to him. During his lifetime, he conquered the Hejaz, the Yemen, and all of the Arabian Peninsula, as well as the areas bordering Syria and Iraq. He brought a fifth of the booty as well as the *jizya*-tax and zakat, of which earlier kings had only obtained a fraction. He was given gifts by several foreign kings. He did not keep any of that for himself, nor did he withhold a single dirham of it. He spent it all in its proper channels, enriched others with it, and strengthened the Muslims by it. He ﷺ said, "I do not feel at ease if a single gold dinar remains in my possession overnight, except for a dinar which I

have set aside to pay a debt."[185]

Sometimes he was given dinars and distributed them, and perhaps six would be left over. Then he would give them to some of his wives. He would not sleep until he had distributed them all. Then he would say, "Now I can rest."[186] When he passed away, his armor was in pawn to feed his family.[187]

As far as his maintenance, clothing, and dwelling were concerned, he was content with the demands of necessity and abstained from anything more than that. He would wear whatever clothing was available; generally, he would wear a cloak (*ridāʾ*), a course garment, or a thick outer garment. He would distribute outer garments made of brocade and embroidered with gold to those who were there and send them to people who were not there. That is because, with the people of Allah, pride in dress and adornment is not one of the qualities of nobility and honor. It is one of the qualities of women. The garments which are most praised are those which are clean and of medium quality. Wearing clothes of this kind does not detract from manliness...

In *al-Mawāhib* it states:

Beauty in physical form, clothing, and appearance is three types: beauty that is praised, beauty that is condemned, and beauty that is neither praised nor condemned.

Praiseworthy beauty is beauty that is for the sake of Allah, and which helps one to obey Allah and

185 Al-Haythamī, *Mawārid al-ẓamʾān*.
186 Ibn Saʿd, *Ṭabaqāt*.
187 Ibn Abī Shayba, *Muṣannaf*.

carry out His commands and respond faithfully to Him. This is seen in how the Prophet ﷺ would beautify himself before receiving delegations. This is comparable to wearing battle attire for the purpose of fighting, or like wearing silk in war in a boastful, vainglorious manner, for that is praiseworthy because it entails making Allah's word supreme and rendering aid to His religion and enraging His enemies.

Condemnable beauty is beauty that is for the sake of the lower world, or for the sake of authority, boastfulness, vainglory, or when it is the servant's most ambitious goal and purpose.

Beauty that is neither praised nor condemned is the beauty that is free of the two aforementioned intentions and without their descriptions. The Prophet ﷺ did not confine himself to a particular type of attire, nor did he seek out what was costly and luxurious; rather, he would wear what was readily available...

Abū Nuʿaym related in *Ḥilyat [al-Awliyāʾ]*, on the authority of Ibn ʿUmar in a raised tradition, "Verily, it is from the nobility of a believer in the sight of Allah (the Exalted and Sublime!) that his garment be clean and that he be satisfied with what is minimal."[188] He also related from the hadith of Jābir that the Prophet ﷺ once saw a man whose garment was dirty, and said, "Could this man not find something with which to clean his garment?"[189] ...

The Prophet's ﷺ manner of dress was such that it is better and more beneficial for the body, and

188 Al-ʿAjlūnī, *Kashf al-khafā*.
189 Abū Nuʿaym, *Ḥilyat al-Awliyāʾ*.

> easier. For his turban was not so large that it would cause him harm by wearing it, or weaken him or impair him—nor was it so small that it could not protect his head from the heat and cold. Likewise with respect to [the Prophet's] over garments and loin cloths, which were less burdensome than other articles of clothing; and he ﷺ did not lengthen and widen his sleeves.

The most beloved article of clothing that the Messenger of Allah ﷺ wore was the shirt (*qamīṣ*).[190] "The word *qamīṣ*," as the author of *al-Qāmūs* [*al-Muḥīṭ*][191] said, "is the name for the woven garment with sleeves and a pocket, which is worn underneath regular clothes, and [is light and] not woolen." The Prophet ﷺ only had one shirt. It is reported that ʿĀʾisha ﷺ said, "The Messenger of Allah ﷺ never took leftovers from lunch or dinner; neither did he possess a pair of anything—he did not own two shirts, or two over garments, or two loin cloths, or two pairs of sandals."

The sleeve of his shirt would reach his wrist. [In another narration] the Prophet's sleeve would reach his fingers.[192]

The Prophet's shirt ﷺ was above his ankles, and his sleeve would reach his fingers.[193]

When the Prophet ﷺ would wear a shirt he would be begin with the right side.

Qurra b. Iyās ﷺ related, "I came to the Messenger of

190 Al-Tirmidhī, *Shamāʾil.*

191 Majd al-Dīn al-Fayrūzabādī. [t]

192 Al-Zabīdī in *Itḥāf al-sādat al-muttaqīn.*

193 Ibid.

Allah ﷺ with a group of people from Muzayna[194] so that we could pledge our fealty to him. The buttons of his shirt were unfastened. I inserted my hand in the opening of his shirt and felt the Seal [of Prophethood]."[195]

The Most beloved of garments to the Messenger of Allah ﷺ was the *ḥibra,* which is an ornate and beautiful Yemeni mantle.[196]

The Prophet ﷺ owned two green mantles with greenish colored stripes. He ﷺ liked green clothing.

Abū Juḥayfa ﷺ reported, "I saw the Prophet ﷺ as he was wearing a red garment. It is as if I am looking at the radiance of his shins now."[197] The word for garment, *ḥulla,* describes a loin cloth and an over garment [together]; something is called a *ḥulla* only if it consists of a loin cloth and an over garment, or a long shirt with an inner lining.

The Prophet ﷺ used to clothe his daughters in silk *khimars*.[198] A *khimar* is a cloth that a woman uses to cover her head.

The Prophet ﷺ would take the silk from garments and remove it.[199]

The value of the Prophet's clothing ﷺ was ten dirhams.

Qayla b. Makhrama ﷺ said, "I saw the Prophet ﷺ and he was wearing two unstitched garments."[200] Anas b. Mālik ﷺ reported, "The Prophet ﷺ once came out while leaning on Usāma [b. Zayd] ﷺ. He had a Yemeni

194 A tribe of Muḍar. [t]
195 Al-Tirmidhī, *Shamāʾil.*
196 Ibid.
197 Ibid.
198 Al-Muttaqī al-Hindī, *Kanz al-ʿummāl.*
199 Aḥmad, *Musnad.*
200 Ibid.

upper garment that was thrown around him. He then led the prayer."[201] This garment, called a *qiṭrī,* was a type of Yemeni mantle made of cotton with a rough texture and red patterns. The phrase "thrown around him" means that he placed it over his shoulders, or that he wrapped around his neck.

ʿĀʾisha ﷺ reported, "The Messenger of Allah ﷺ went out one morning wearing a long and wide cloak made of black hair."[202]

Mughīra b. Shuʿba ﷺ reported that the Prophet ﷺ once wore a long Roman *jubba* that had tight sleeves.[203] A *jubba* is an outer garment made of two garments stitched together with padded lining inside. It can also be a single garment with no padding inside if its outer portion is woolen.

The Prophet's sleeves ﷺ reached his wrists. He would wear an outer garment that was open from the front, as well as a cloak. He would also wear an outer garment with tight sleeves when on a journey.[204]

It is related that Asmāʾ b. Abī Bakr ﷺ once took out a printed Persian cloak that had a hem of brocade along the pockets and a split from the front and the back bordered with brocade. She said, "This is the cloak of the Messenger of Allah ﷺ. It was with ʿĀʾisha ﷺ, and when she passed away I took possession of it. The Prophet ﷺ used to wear this, and now we wash it for the sick and seek a cure from it."[205]

The Messenger of Allah ﷺ would wear whatever

201 Ibid.
202 Al-ʿUqaylī, *al-Ḍuʿafāʾ*.
203 Al-Tirmidhī, *Shamāʾil.*
204 Ibid.
205 Muslim, *Ṣaḥīḥ*.

he could find. Sometimes he would wear a *shamla* (a small garment that is wrapped around the body), and sometimes he would wear a *ḥibra,* and sometimes he would wear a woolen outer garment—whatever he could find of permissible clothing then he would wear it.

Abū Mūsā al-Ashʿarī ﷺ said, "ʿĀʾisha ﷺ brought out for us a patched upper garment and a coarse loin cloth, and said, 'The Messenger of Allah ﷺ passed on while wearing these two garments.'"[206]

The Prophet ﷺ owned a patched over garment, and would say, "I am but a servant; I dress as a servant dresses."[207]

The Prophet ﷺ also owned a black over garment that he gifted to someone. Umm Salama ﷺ said to him, "Whatever happened to that black garment?" He ﷺ replied, "I gifted it to someone." She said, "I never saw anything as beautiful as your radiance contrasted with its blackness!"[208]

The Prophet ﷺ would sometimes wrap himself with his shawl, and sometimes he would leave it [hanging loose]—which is called a *ṭaylasān* according to custom.

Most of what the Prophet ﷺ and his Companions would wear were stitched cotton garments, though occasionally they would wear stitched woolen or linen garments.

The Prophet ﷺ wore a garment made of black hair, and once wore a woolen mantle—though he could smell the odor of the sheep on it so he casted it off.

The Messenger of Allah owned a pair of pants (*sarāwīl*),

206 Al-Tibrīzī, *Mishkāt al-maṣābīḥ*.

207 Al-Zabīdī, *Itḥāf al-sādāt al-muttaqīn*.

208 Ibid.

and he wore a pair of sandals known as *tāsuma*.[209]

The Prophet ﷺ had a sheet (*mulāʾa*) dyed with saffron that would accompany him whenever he went to visit his wives. Whomever he would sleep with would unfurl it and sprinkle water on it, which would bring out the smell of saffron from it. He would sleep in this sheet with his wives.

The Prophet ﷺ had a cloth wrap dyed with saffron. Sometimes he would lead people in the prayer wearing it alone, and sometimes he would wear only a single covering and nothing else.[210]

The Prophet ﷺ would sometimes pray during the night wearing a loin cloth. He would cover himself with part of it and place the rest of it over one of his wives [as she slept], and would pray in this manner.

The Prophet's clothes ﷺ were all above his ankles, and his loin cloth was even higher, at mid-shin level. His shirt would be fastened, and sometimes, during prayer and other occasions, he would unfasten it.

ʿUbayd b. Khālid ﷺ reported, "Once when I was walking in Medina a person behind me said, 'Lift up your loin cloth, for it is more pious and cleaner!' Lo and behold it was the Messenger of Allah ﷺ, so I replied, 'O Messenger of Allah! It is only a *burda malḥāʾ* [a black wrap with white stitching, worn by the Arabs and not considered fancy].' He said, 'Do you not have me as your exemplar?'—and then I looked and saw that his loin cloth was at his mid-shin level."[211]

Salama b. al-Akwaʿ ﷺ reported, "ʿUthmān b. ʿAffān

209 *Tāsuma* sandals are a type of sandal that covers some of the toes and the front of the foot. [t]

210 Al-Zabīdī, *Itḥāf al-sādāt al-muttaqīn*.

211 Aḥmad, *Musnad*.

ﷺ would wear his loin cloth at mid-shin level. He would say, 'This is how the loin cloth of my Companion was'—meaning the Prophet ﷺ."[212]

Ḥudhayfa b. al-Yamān ﷺ reported, "The Prophet ﷺ once took hold of my calf muscle and said, 'This where the loin cloth should reach. If you refuse, then let it be lower. And if you refuse, [then know] that the loin cloth has no right being below the ankles.'"[213]

Ibn ᶜUmar ﷺ related, "The Prophet ﷺ once saw me with my loin cloth dragging [below my ankles] and said to me, 'O Ibn ᶜUmar! Every garment that touches the earth is in the Hellfire!'"[214]

Abū Hurayra ﷺ related that the Prophet ﷺ said, "Whatever of the loin cloth that is below the ankles is in the Hellfire."[215] This is interpreted by the other reports that qualify it, in which the severe threat applies the one who does it out of pride.

The Prophet ﷺ would have the front part of his loin cloth hang low, and would lift up the back of it.[216]

When the Prophet ﷺ would acquire a new garment he would name it—whether a shirt, a turban, or over garment—and then say, "O Allah, to You is all praise. You have clothed me in this; I ask You of its good and the good for which it was made, and I seek refuge in You from its evil and the evil for which it was made."[217]

When the Prophet ﷺ would wear a new garment he would praise Allah Most High, pray two units of prayer,

212 Al-Tirmidhī, *Shamāʾil.*

213 Ibid.

214 Aḥmad, *Musnad.*

215 Al-Bukhārī, *Ṣaḥīḥ.*

216 Al-Zabīdī, *Itḥāf al-sādāt al-muttaqīn.*

217 Al-Tirmidhī, *Shamāʾil.*

and then put on an older garment (*kasā al-khalaq*).[218]

When the Prophet ﷺ would acquire a new garment, he would wear it [first] on a Friday.[219]

The Prophet ﷺ had a mantle that he would wear on the two Eids and on Fridays.[220] He ﷺ would wear a red mantle every Eid.[221] And [in another narration] he would wear a *Ḥibra*[222] mantle every Eid.[223]

ʿUmar b. al-Khaṭṭāb ؓ was once with the Prophet ﷺ and the two of them passed by the market place. ʿUmar saw an silk embroidered shirt and said, "O Messenger of Allah! You should take this [to wear] on Eid!" The Messenger of Allah ﷺ said, "This is only worn by one who has no portion of [it] the Hereafter."[224]

On the day of Eid the Companions (may Allah be pleased with them all) would dress their sons in the finest clothes they could find, as well as dyed garments.

Besides his normal daily attire, the Prophet ﷺ had two garments reserved for Fridays. Sometimes he would wear a loin cloth by itself, whose end corners he would take and tie at the top between his shoulders. Sometimes he would lead funeral prayers wearing just a loin cloth, and sometimes he would pray at home wearing a single loin cloth with its corners folded over—and that would

218 Al-Haythamī, *Majmaʿ al-zawāʾid*. In other words, he would take off the new garment, put on an older one, and give the new one away in charity. [t]

219 Al-Zabīdī, *Itḥāf al-sādāt al-muttaqīn*.

220 Ibid.

221 Abū al-Shaykh, *Ahklāq al-Nubuwwa*.

222 A striped Yemeni mantle. [t]

223 Al-Bayhaqī, *al-Sunan al-kubrā*.

224 Al-Bukhārī, *Ṣaḥīḥ*.

be the loin cloth he used that day when having intimate relations [with one of his wives].[225]

When a delegation would come to see the Prophet ﷺ, he would wear his best garments and instruct his Companions to do the same.[226]

The Prophet's over garment was six cubits and a hand span[227], and his loin cloth was four and a hand span[228] in length and six cubits and a hand span in width.[229]

The Prophet ﷺ would wear mantles that had red stitching, and he used to forbid his Companions from wearing solid red garments.

Ibn ʿAbbās ؓ related, "The Messenger of Allah ﷺ said, 'Wear white clothing. Let your living wear them and use them to shroud your dead, for indeed white is the best of your clothing.'"[230]

In *al-Mawāhib* it states: "It is reported from ʿUrwa, 'The length of the Prophet's over garment was four cubits, and its width was two cubits and a hand span.'" [Then the author of *al-Mawāhib* stated:]

A SUBTLE POINT

It is said that since there is nothing from the Messenger of Allah ﷺ except that it is pure, a sign of that purity on his blessed body is that none of his garments ever became dirty—and it is [also] said that they never became lice-infested. Ibn Sabʿ said in *al-Shifā,* and al-Sabtī said in *Aʿdhab al-Mawārid wa Aṭyab al-Mawālid,*

225 Al-Zabīdī, *Itḥāf al-Sāda al-Muttaqīn.*
226 Al-Muttaqī al-Hindī, *Kanz al-ʿUmmāl.*
227 Approximately 300 centimeters. [t]
228 Approximately 350 centimeters in length. [t]
229 Approximately 110 centimeters. [t]
230 Al-Tirmidhī, *Shamāʾil.*

that lice, out of reverence and honor for the Prophet ﷺ, never bothered him. Al-Fakhr al-Rāzī also relates that flies never landed on his clothing, and that mosquitoes never sucked his blood.

The Messenger of Allah ﷺ would wear a white *qalansuwa*.[231] A *qalansuwa* is a cap.[232] The Prophet ﷺ would wear a *qalansuwa* under [his] turban, or without a turban, and sometimes he would wear a turban without a *qalansuwa*. He would wear white Yemeni *qalansuwa*s that had stuffing inside of them, and during times of war he would wear a *qalansuwa* that had an ear covering.[233] The Prophet ﷺ would sometimes remove his *qalansuwa* and place it before him as a barrier during prayer (*sutra*). Sometimes the Prophet ﷺ did not have a turban to wear, and so he would tie a cloth around his head and forehead.

When the Prophet would tie his turban he would let its tail hang between his shoulders.[234] The Prophet ﷺ would wrap his turban around his head and insert the tail behind his head and let it hang between his shoulders.[235] When he would tie his turban, the Prophet ﷺ would let it hang between his shoulders, though at times he would draw it close and tuck it in, and at other times he would only let part of it hang out.[236] The Prophet ﷺ would

231 Al-Haythamī, *Majmaʿ al-zawāʾid*.
232 What we would call today a kufi or a topee. [t]
233 Al-Zabīdī, *Itḥāf al-sādat al-muttaqīn*.
234 Al-Tirmidhī, *Shamāʾil*.
235 Al-Muttaqī al-Hindī, *Kanz al-ʿummāl*.
236 From this narration we understand that the Prophet ﷺ would either keep the tail of the turban between his shoulders,

often wind the turban under his chin (*taḥt al-ḥanak*) as is the way of the North Africans.

The Prophet ﷺ had a turban named *saḥāb* [literally, "clouds"] that he gifted to ʿAlī ؓ. At times ʿAlī would come out wearing it and the Prophet ﷺ would say, "ʿAlī has come to you among the clouds!"[237] ʿAlī ؓ reported, "The Messenger of Allah ﷺ wrapped a turban around my head and hung its tail between my shoulders. He said [to me], 'Verily Allah supported me during the battles of Badr and Ḥunayn with angels wearing turbans wrapped in this manner.'"[238]

The Prophet ﷺ also said, "Verily the turban is the distinguishing mark that differentiates between the Muslims and the idol-worshippers."[239]

The Prophet ﷺ would not appoint a leader until he tied a turban around the man's head and hung its tail on his right side near his ear.[240]

Jābir ؓ reported, "The Messenger of Allah ﷺ entered Mecca on the day of conquest wearing a black turban."[241]

Ibn Ḥajar al-Makkī said, "Know, as some of the hadith masters have said, that all of the reports about the length and width of the Prophet's turban have not been ascertained authoritatively (*lam yuḥarrar*)."[242]

---

tuck it in, or have one part of it between his shoulders and the other part over his shoulder. [t]

237 Al-Zabīdī, *Itḥāf al-sādat al-muttaqīn*.

238 Ibn Abī Shayba, *Muṣannaf*.

239 Al-Bayhaqī, *al-Sunan al-kubrā*.

240 Al-Ṭabarānī, *al-Muʿjam al-kabīr*.

241 Al-Tirmidhī, *Shamāʾil*.

242 That is, the reports about the exact length of the Prophet's turban are of questionable authenticity and insufficient for establishing it with any degree of authority. Al-Suyūṭī and others mentioned some reports that say it was between seven and ten cubits

The Messenger of Allah ﷺ had a cloth with which he would wipe himself after ablutions.[243] He would use the bottom of his foot to wipe.[244]

in length, or approximately 336–480 centimeters. [t]

243 Al-Baghawī, *Sharḥ al-Sunna.*

244 Al-Ghazālī, *Iḥyāʾ ʿulūm al-dīn.* Al-Ḥāfiẓ al-ʿIraqī comments, "I do not know of this being his practice. What is known, however, is mentioned in the *Sunan* of Ibn Mājah from the hadith of Jābir ؓ who said, 'During the time of the Messenger of Allah ﷺ we seldom found food; and when we did find food we seldom had handkerchiefs with which to wipe ourselves; we only had our hands and arms.'" [t]

SECTION TWO

The Description of the Prophet's Bedding & Related Matters ﷺ

THE MESSENGER OF Allah ﷺ had a bedding from tanned skin with palm-tree fiber as its stuffing. Its length was around two cubits, and its width was around one cubit and a hand span.

ʿĀʾisha ﷺ was asked, "What was the bedding of the Messenger of Allah ﷺ?" She replied, "It was made from tanned skin, and its stuffing was of palm-tree fiber."[245] ʿĀʾisha ﷺ also reported, "A woman from the Helpers came to visit me and she saw that the bedding of the Messenger of Allah ﷺ was but a coarse cover. She later sent me a bedding stuffed with wool. Soon thereafter the Messenger of Allah ﷺ came in upon me and asked, 'What is this, ʿĀʾisha?' I replied, 'O Messenger of Allah! So-and-so, the Anṣārī woman, came by and saw your bedding and then sent this to me.' He ﷺ said, 'Send it back, ʿĀʾisha, for by Allah, had I so wished, Allah would have sent to me mountains of gold and silver!'"[246]

Ḥafṣa ﷺ was asked, "What was the bedding of the Messenger of Allah ﷺ in your home?" She replied, "A coarse woolen blanket that we would fold in half and

245 Al-Tirmidhī, *Shamāʾil*.
246 Al-Zabīdī, *Itḥāf al-sādat al-muttaqīn*.

spread out for him to sleep upon. One night I said to myself, 'If I folded it four times it will be more comfortable for him'—and so I folded it four times. When the Messenger of Allah ﷺ woke up the next morning he asked, 'What did you spread out for me last night?' I replied, 'Your bedding, except I folded it four times and said to myself that it would be more comfortable for you.' He said, 'Refold it as it was before, for its softness prevented me from praying in the night [for the night vigil prayer].'"[247]

The Prophet ﷺ had a cloak that would be spread out for him wherever he went. It would be folded twice underneath him. The Prophet ﷺ would often sleep only on a palm mat with nothing else underneath it. ʿAbdullāh b. Masʿūd ؓ reported, "I once went to see the Prophet ﷺ as he was in a room [that was so hot it was] like a bath. He was sleeping on a palm mat that had left its imprint on his side. Seeing this, I began to cry, and [when he woke up] he asked me, 'What causes you to cry, ʿAbdullāh?' I replied, 'O Messenger of Allah! Chosroes and Caesar sleep comfortably upon silken beddings and here you are sleeping on this palm mat that has left marks on you!' The Messenger of Allah ﷺ replied, 'Do not cry, ʿAbdullāh, for they have the lower world and we have the Hereafter!'"[248]

Ibn ʿAbbās ؓ reported that Umar b. al-Khaṭṭāb related, "I went to see the Messenger of Allah ﷺ and he was lying upon a palm mat. I sat down and saw that he was wearing a loin cloth and nothing more, and saw that the palm mat had left an imprint upon his side. I saw

247 Al-Tirmidhī, *Shamāʾil*.
248 Al-Ṭabarānī, *al-Muʿjam al-kabīr*.

there about a *ṣāʿ*[249] of barley and an untanned animal skin hanging [on the wall]. Seeing this sight my eyes welled up with tears. The Messenger of Allah ﷺ asked me, 'What makes you cry, O son of al-Khaṭṭāb?' I replied, 'O Prophet of Allah! How can I not cry when this palm mat has left an imprint on your side, and here is your provision that I see is so scant, while Chosroes and Caesar enjoy fruits and flowing rivers, and you are the Prophet of Allah and His Chosen One yet these are your possessions!' The Prophet ﷺ said, 'O son of al-Khaṭṭāb! Are you not pleased that we have the Hereafter and they have this lower world? They are a folk for whom the fine things of this world have been hastened and given, and they are bound to vanish, while we are a folk whose fine things are delayed to our Hereafter.'"[250]

ʿĀʾisha ﷺ said, "The Messenger of Allah ﷺ had a bed made of woven *bardī*[251] with a black covering over it. We had stuffed it with *bardī*, and when Abū Bakr came in he saw the Prophet ﷺ sleeping on it. When the Prophet woke and saw us he rose and sat up. We looked at him and saw the markings from the bed imprinted on his side. We said, 'O Messenger of Allah, we see that the roughness of your bedding and cover is harming you, yet the Chosroes and Caesar sleep on beds of silk and embroidery!' The Prophet ﷺ said, 'Do not say that, for the beddings of the Chosroes and Caesar shall be fire. The reward for my bedding and covering is the Garden!'"[252]

The Messenger of Allah ﷺ never found fault with a bedding. When a bed was prepared for him he would lie

249 Around two liters. [t]
250 Al-Ḥākim, *al-Mustadrak*.
251 A type of plant whose leaves are used for weaving. [t]
252 Ibn Ḥibbān, *Ṣaḥīḥ*.

upon it, and if there was no bedding to be had he would lie on the ground.

The Messenger of Allah ﷺ would cover himself with a *liḥāf* [253] [when sleeping]. He ﷺ said to his wives, "Jibrīl never came to me while covered in a *liḥāf* belonging to any of you—except for ʿĀʾisha's."

The cushion that the Prophet ﷺ used to recline on was filled with palm fiber stuffing.[254]

Jābir b. Samura said, "I saw the Prophet ﷺ while he was reclining on a cushion on his left side."[255]

The Prophet ﷺ would offer his prayers on a palm mat.[256]

The Prophet ﷺ would [also] offer his prayers on a *bisāṭ*.[257]

The Prophet ﷺ liked to have a hairless leather mat on which to pray.[258]

253 A *liḥāf* is a thin sheet like covering used as a head covering or a sheet. [t]

254 Aḥmad, *Musnad*.

255 Al-Tirmidhī, *Shamāʾil*.

256 Al-Munāwī, *Kunūz al-ḥaqāʾiq*.

257 Ibn Mājah, *Sunan*. A *bisāṭ* is another word for mat, although it can be made from palm fronds or other materials. [t]

258 Ibn Saʿd, *Ṭabaqāt*.

SECTION THREE

The Description of the Prophet's Ring ﷺ

THE RING OF the Messenger of Allah ﷺ was silver (*wariq*) and its stone (*faṣṣ*) was Abyssinian.[259] The *faṣṣ* is the part on which the owner's name is written. It was of onyx, which is a stone containing a mixture of black and white, or it was carnelian (*ʿaqīq*), whose mines are located in Abyssinia. It is not reported that the Prophet ﷺ ever wore a ring made entirely of carnelian. The Prophet's ring ﷺ was silver and its stone was part of it.[260]

Ibn ʿUmar ﷺ reported that the Prophet ﷺ had taken for himself a ring of silver that he would use to stamp letters but did not wear it.[261]

The Prophet ﷺ would wear his ring on his right hand.[262] Al-Bājūrī said, "Wearing a ring on the left hand is neither offensive (*makrūh*) nor against what is best (*khilāf al-awlā*). On the contrary, it is a Sunna by virtue of being reported in several rigorously authenticated hadith. Nevertheless, it is better to wear a ring on the

259 Al-Tirmidhī, *Shamāʾil*.

260 Ibid. This means the stone was imbedded as part of the ring and not separate from it. [t]

261 Ibid.

262 Ibid.

right hand because the hadith reports concerning it are more authentic."

The Prophet ﷺ would [also] wear his ring on his left hand.[263]

The Prophet ﷺ would take the stone [top part] of his ring and turn it inward towards his palm.[264]

The engraving on the ring of the Messenger of Allah ﷺ was such that one line had *Muḥammad*, the line above it had *Rasūl*, and the line above it had *Allāh*.[265]

Allāh
Rasūl
Muḥammad

Anas b. Mālik ؓ reported, "When the Messenger of Allah ﷺ wanted to write to the non-Arabs[266] he was informed that they only accept letters that are marked with stamps, so he had a ring made. It is as if I am looking at its whiteness in his palm now."[267]

Anas ؓ also reported, "The Prophet ﷺ wrote to the Chosroes, the Caesar, and the Negus. He was told that they do not accept letters unless they are marked with stamps, so he had a ring made for him. Its hoop was silver, and engraved upon it was *Muḥammad the Messenger of Allah*."[268]

263 Ibid.
264 Ibid.
265 Ibid.
266 That is, to write to their rulers to invite them to Islam. [t]
267 Al-Tirmidhī, *Shamāʾil*.
268 Ibid.

The Prophet ﷺ would stamp letters and say, "Stamping a letter is better than suspicion."[269]

Ibn ʿUmar ؓ reported, "The Messenger of Allah ﷺ had taken a gold ring for himself that he would wear on his right hand. People then began taking gold rings for themselves. [Upon seeing this] the Messenger of Allah threw the ring away[270] and said, 'I shall never wear it again.' The people then threw their rings away, too."[271]

Ibn ʿUmar ؓ also reported, "The Prophet ﷺ had taken a silver ring for himself and would turn its stone inward towards his palm. Engraved upon it was *Muḥammad the Messenger of Allah*, and he forbade anyone from having the same engraving. This is the same ring that fell from [the hand of] Muʿayqīb in the ʿArīs Well."[272] Muʿayqīb was from the participants at the Battle of Badr and was the keeper of the ring of the Chosen One [the Prophet] ﷺ and the Caliphs after him.[273]

ʿAbdullāh b. ʿUmar ؓ [also] reported, "The Messenger of Allah ﷺ had taken a silver ring for himself. It was in his hand, and then in the hand of Abū Bakr, and then the hand of ʿUmar, and then the hand of ʿUthmān, till it fell into the Well of ʿArīs. Engraved upon it was *Muḥammad the Messenger of Allah*."[274]

269 Al-Zabīdī, *Itḥāf al-sādat al-muttaqīn*.
270 At the moment Allah revealed to him that men are to be forbidden from wearing gold. [t]
271 Al-Tirmidhī, *Shamāʾil*.
272 Ibid.
273 That is, he was responsible for carrying the ring when the Prophet ﷺ was not wearing it, and he was also responsible for carrying it during the reigns of Abū Bakr, ʿUmar, and ʿUthmān. [t]
274 Al-Tirmidhī, *Shamāʿil*.

Al-Bājūrī said:

> Its fall [into the well] was a subtle indication that the Caliphate was conditioned upon it, for [after its fall] there came successive tribulations, disunity, and wanton killing. It is for this reason that some have said that the ring of the Messenger of Allah ﷺ contained secrets like the ring of Sulaymān, for when Sulaymān's ring was lost so too was his kingdom; and likewise when ʿUthmān lost the Prophet's ring ﷺ his authority soon weakened and discord arose (which led ultimately to his murder), which will continue till the end of time.

When the Prophet ﷺ wanted to remind himself about an important matter lest he forget it, he would tie a small string around his pinky finger or around his ring.[275]

Anas reported, "When the Prophet ﷺ would enter the privy he would remove his ring."[276]

A man once came wearing a brass ring—another narration has it, "wearing a ring of *ṣufr*," which is a type of copper that was used in the construction of idols—and the Prophet ﷺ said to him, "Why is it that I smell the odor of idols from you?" The man immediately threw it away. Later, the same man came wearing an iron ring and the Prophet said to him, "Why is it that see on you the adornment of the denizens of Hell?" The man immediately threw it away. The man asked, "O Messenger of Allah, from what should I take as a ring?"

275 Ibn Saʿd, *Ṭabaqāt*.
276 Al-Tirmidhī, *Shamāʾil*.

The Prophet ﷺ replied, "From silver, but make it no more than a *mithqāl*[277] in weight."[278]

277 A *mithqāl* equals the weight of an Islamic dinar, which is either 4.231 grams or 4.46 grams. [t]
278 Abū Dāwūd, *Sunan*.

SECTION FOUR

The Description of the Prophet's Sandals & Leather Socks ﷺ

THE SANDALS OF the Messenger of Allah ﷺ had two toe-straps and two mid-foot straps.[279] [Al-Bājūrī said:] A strap (*qibāl*) is a cord-like material placed between the middle toe and the third toe. The Prophet ﷺ would place one strap between his big toe and second toe, and the second strap between his middle [third] toe and fourth toe. A mid-foot strap is a strap that runs along the top of the foot.

Ibn ʿUmar ﷺ would wear *sibtī* sandals, which are hairless leather sandals. He said, "I saw the Messenger of Allah ﷺ wear hairless sandals and perform ablutions in them, and so I love to wear them, too."[280]

ʿAmr b. Ḥurayth ﷺ said, "I saw the Messenger of Allah ﷺ pray in sandals that had new soles sewn onto the old."[281]

Jābir b. ʿAbdullāh ﷺ said, "The Prophet ﷺ forbade eating with the left hand as well as walking with only one sandal."[282]

279 Al-Tirmidhī, *Shamāʾil*.
280 Ibid.
281 Ibid.
282 Ibid.

Abū Hurayra ﷺ reported that the Prophet ﷺ said, "When one of you puts on his sandals let him begin with the right [sandal], and when he doffs his sandals let him begin with the left [sandal]—let the right sandal be the first one on and the last one doffed."[283]

When the Prophet ﷺ would sit down to converse [with others] he would doff his Sandals.[284]

Al-Bājūrī said, "The Prophet's Sandals ﷺ were *mukhaṣṣara, muᶜaqqaba,* and *mulassanna,* as Ibn Saᶜd recorded in the *Ṭabaqāt.*" *Mukhaṣṣara* means they were somewhat narrow in the middle. *Muᶜaqqaba* means they had heel straps made of leather that would hold the back of the foot in place. *Mulassanna* means that their front portion extended out in the shape of a tongue.

The great hadith-master Zayn al-Dīn al-ᶜIrāqī (may Allah have mercy upon him) said in his thousand line didactic poem on the Prophetic Biography (*Alfiyya al-Sīra al-Nabawiyya*), may the finest prayers and peace be upon its subject:

And his noble and sanctified Sandals—
Glad tidings to the one who touches them with his brow!
They each have two toe-straps and mid-foot straps
Hairless, all their hair having been removed
In length they are a hand-span and two fingers;
In width, the distance between the [lateral] and [medial] ankles,
Seven fingers in width, and the mid-foot five fingers
In width, and above the mid-foot six fingers—know this

283 Ibid.

284 Al-Bayhaqī, *Shuᶜab al-īmān.*

The front of the sandals are shorter [in width], and
the width
Between the two straps are two fingers—calculate them
This is a description of those Sandals
And how noble they are indeed!

BENEFIT

[Al-Qasṭalānī] said in *al-Mawāhib,* "Ibn ʿAsākir devoted an entire volume to the image of the Prophet's Sandals ﷺ, as did others, such as Abū Isḥāq Ibrāhīm b. Muḥammad b. Khalaf al-Sulamī al-Andalūsī and others... Because the Sandals are so well-known and because of the difficulty of accurately measuring their size (except for one who is skilled) I did not reproduce them here."

Some of the virtues of the Sandals that have been mentioned, and some of their benefits and blessings that are tried and true, include the following: It is recorded that Abū Jaʿfar Aḥmad b. ʿAbd al-Majīd (who was a righteous shaykh) had given some of his students replica images of the Sandal. Soon thereafter one of the students went to him and said, "From the blessings of the Sandal I was witness to the most astounding thing last night! My wife was suffering intense pain and was on the verge of death, so I took the image of the Sandal and placed on the site of her pain and supplicated, 'O Allah, show me the blessings of the owner of this Sandal!' Right then, immediately after I supplicated, Allah healed her!"

Abū Isḥāq said, "Abū al-Qāsim b. Muḥammad said, 'Of the tried and true blessings of the Sandal is that whoever holds it for the sake of seeking blessings will have protection from the harms of transgressors and the overpowering of enemies, and it will serve as a protection from every insolent devil and envious eye; and if a woman in labor holds onto it in her right hand, her delivery will be made easy, by Allah's strength and power.'"

How excellent is the statement of Abū Bakr al-Qurṭubī (may Allah Most High have mercy upon him):

Out of awe for the Sandal's splendor, we humbled ourselves before it
For as long as we humble ourselves before it we will be elevated!
So place it on the top of your head, for in reality
It is a crown whose form is that of a Sandal!
By the sole of the Best of Creation, it is superior
To any crown, such that [his] foot surpasses the parting line of the head!
It is a healing for the sick, a hope for the suffering
A security for the frightened—such are its virtues!

Burayda ﷺ reported, "The Negus gifted the Prophet ﷺ two black leather socks. The Prophet ﷺ put them on and then performed ablutions and wiped over them."[285]

Al-Mughīra b. Shuʿba ﷺ said, "Diḥya gifted the Prophet ﷺ a pair of leather socks which the Prophet then wore."[286]

Al-Ṭabarānī narrated in his [*al-Muʿjam*] *al-awsaṭ* on the authority of the erudite [ʿAbdullāh Ibn ʿAbbās ﷺ] who said, "When the Messenger of Allah ﷺ wanted to answer the call of nature he would walk away for some distance. One day he went out to answer the call of nature, and after he finished he performed ablutions and put on one of his leather socks, when suddenly a green bird swooped down and took the other sock and flew up

285 Al-Tirmidhī, *Shamāʾil.*
286 Ibid.

with it and then dropped it down, and lo there slithered out of it a black snake. The Prophet ﷺ said, "This is a noble gift that Allah has blessed me with. O Allah, I seek refuge in You from the evil of those who crawl on their bellies, the evil of those who walk on two feet, and the evil of those who walk on four!'"[287]

287 Al-Ṭabarānī, *al-Muʿjam al-awsaṭ*.

SECTION FIVE

The Description of the Prophet's Weapons ﷺ

[MUḤAMMAD] IBN Sīrīn said, "I had my sword made on the model of Samura b. Jundub's sword ﷺ, as he said that he had his made on the model of the Prophet's sword ﷺ. The Prophet's sword ﷺ was of *ḥanafī* make." *Ḥanafī* here is an ascription to the Banū Ḥanīfa tribe, who were well known for their expertise as bladesmiths.

Anas ﷺ said, "The grip of the sword of Allah's Messenger was of silver."[288]

Jaʿfar b. Muḥammad related on the authority of his father [Muḥammad al-Bāqir] that "The pommel, guard, and grip of the sword of Allah's Messenger were of silver."

The Prophet ﷺ had numerous swords. They include:

Al-Maʾthūr, which was his first sword, inherited from his father

Al-Qaḍīb

Al-Qalaʿī (or al-Qulaʿī), in ascription to a remote desert area named Qalaʿ

Al-Battār ("The Cutter")

Al-Ḥatf ("Death")

288 Al-Tirmidhī, *Shamāʾil.*

Al-Mikh'dham ("The Slicer")
Al-Rasūb ("The Plunging Blade")
Al-Ṣamṣāma ("The Unbreakable Blade")
Al-Laḥīf ("The Enveloper")
Dhū al-Fiqār (or Dhū al-Faqār)[289]

The scholars have mentioned that one of the Prophet's miracles ﷺ was that he gave ʿUkkāsha [b. Miḥṣan] a wooden club when the latter's sword had broken during the Battle of Badr. He ﷺ said to him "Strike with it" and at that moment the club turned into a long, bright, and sharp sword. ʿUkkāsha went on to fight with it and continued to use it in subsequent battles till he was martyred.[290]

During the Battle of Uḥud the Prophet ﷺ gave ʿAbdullāh b. Jaḥsh a palm branch after his sword had broken. When ʿAbdullāh b. Jaḥsh took hold of the branch it transmuted into a sword.

The Prophet ﷺ had a lance that would be carried for him, and when prayed he would plant it into the ground in front of him.[291]

289 Dhū al-Fiqār was the most famous of the Prophet's swords ﷺ and the sword he carried during the conquest of Mecca. It is said that Dhū al-Fiqār had originally belonged to Prophet Sulaymān ﷺ and was one of six swords gifted to him by Bilqīs Queen of Sheba. Dhū al-Fiqār was later passed down to ʿĀṣ b. Munabbih b. al-Ḥujjāj, who was slain at Badr by Imam ʿAlī b. Abī Ṭālib ﷺ. [t]
290 Al-Bayhaqī, *Dalāʾil al-Nubuwwa.*
291 Al-Ṭabarānī, *al-Muʿjam al-kabīr.*

The Prophet's battle standard (*rāya*) was black, and his flag (*liwāʾ*)[292] was white.[293]

Zubayr b. al-ʿAwwām ﷺ said, "During the Battle of Uḥud the Prophet ﷺ was wearing two pieces of armor. He tried to climb upon a rock but was unable to[294], so he ordered Ṭalḥa to sit by the rock and climbed [upon him] and climbed up to the top of the rock. I heard the Prophet ﷺ say, 'Ṭalḥa has made it incumbent!'"[295] This means Ṭalḥa did an act that made it incumbent for him to enter Paradise.

The Prophet ﷺ had seven pieces of armor. They were named:

Dhāt al-Fuḍūl ("The One of Plenty")—named so because of its size

Dhāt al-Wishāḥ ("The Sash")

Dhāt al-Ḥawāshī ("The One of Retinues")

Fiḍḍa ("Silver")

Al-Sughdiyya (it is said that this plate of armor was the one worn by Prophet Dāwūd ﷺ when he fought against Jālūt (Goliath))

Al-Batrāʾ ("The Short One")

Al-Khizniq ("The Kit"—named after the young child of a rabbit)[296]

292 The difference between a *rāya* and a *liwāʾ* is that the former is used during battles and the latter is hoisted over one's territory or campsite. [t]

293 Al-Baghawī, *Sharḥ al-Sunna*.

294 It is said that the Prophet ﷺ was "unable" because of the weight of the armor on him, or because of his blessed blood flowing on his face, or because of the high elevation. Allah knows best. [t]

295 Al-Tirmidhī, *Shamāʾil*.

296 Al-Zabīdī, *Itḥāf al-sādāt al-muttaqīn*.

Anas b. Mālik said, "The Prophet entered Mecca wearing a *mighfar*."[297] A *mighfar* is a metal helmet made in the shape of one's head. It is fitted under one's cap.

297 Al-Tirmidhī, *Shamāʾil*.

SECTION SIX

It Was from the Character of the Prophet ﷺ to Name His Weapons, Mounts, & Personal Belongings

THE NAME OF the Prophet's battle standard was al-ʿUqāb.[298] It was black, although on one occasion he made it yellow, and on another occasion he made it white with black lines.

The name of his tent was al-Kinn.

The name of his stick (*qaḍīb*) was al-Mamshūq.

The name of his drinking vessel was al-Rayyān.

His drinking cup was named al-Ṣādir. His stirrup was named al-Rājj. His scissors were named al-Jāmiʿ. The sword that he would take into battles was named Dhū al-Fiqār (and he had other swords). He had a leather belt with three silver rings in it.

The name of his quiver was al-Kāfūr. The name of his she-camel was al-Qaṣwāʾ, and it was the one also called al-ʿAḍbāʾ. The name of his mule was al-Duldul. The name of his donkey was Yaʿfūr. The name of his ewe from which he would drink milk was Ghaytha.

In another hadith it is stated that the Prophet ﷺ had

298 Abū al-Shaykh, *Akhlāq al-Nubuwwa*.

an ornamented sword whose grip, pommel, and guard were all silver. It was named Dhū al-Fiqār.

The Prophet ﷺ had a bow named Dhū al-Sadād. He had a quiver named Dhū al-Jumʿ. He had piece of armor inlaid with brass named Dhāt al-Fuḍūl. He had a lance named al-Nabʿāʾ. He had a shield named al-Dhafn (or al-Dhaqn). He had a pure red horse named al-Murtajiz. He had a black horse named al-Sakb. He had a stirrup named al-Rājj. He had a silver mule named al-Duldul. He had a she-camel named al-Qaṣwā, a donkey named Yaʿfūr, a carpet named al-Kazz, and goat named al-Nimr, a drinking cup named al-Ṣādir, a mirror named al-Mudilla (the Guide), a pair of scissors named al-Jāmiʿ, and a stick from a Shawḥaṭ tree[299] name al-Mamshūq.

The Prophet ﷺ had a bag in which he would store a mirror, a comb, a pair of scissors, and a tooth-stick.

The Prophet ﷺ had a horse named al-Laḥīf, another named al-Ẓarib, and another name al-Lizāz.

The Prophet ﷺ had a large dining bowl named al-Gharrāʾ that required four men to carry. The Prophet ﷺ also had a female servant named Khaḍra.[300]

299 A desert tree that grows in the mountains and whose branches are often used to make walking sticks and canes. [t]
300 Al-Zabīdī, *Itḥāf al-sādāt al-muttaqīn*.

Chapter Four

THE DESCRIPTION OF THE EATING, DRINKING, & SLEEPING OF THE PROPHET ﷺ

SECTION ONE

The Description of the Prophet's Lifestyle & Bread ﷺ

SIMĀK B. ḤARB reported, "I heard al-Nuʿmān b. Bashīr ﷺ say, 'Do you not indulge in food and drink as much as you like? Verily, I have seen your Prophet ﷺ at times unable to find even the lowest quality of dates with which to fill his stomach!'"[301]

The Messenger of Allah ﷺ would mostly consume dates and water. ʿĀʾisha ﷺ said, "We, the Family of Muḥammad, would remain for an entire month without ever kindling a fire [to cook food]—there were only dates and water to consume."[302]

In the narration of al-Bukhārī and Muslim, ʿĀʾisha ﷺ said to ʿUrwa, "By Allah, dear nephew, we would see the new moon, then another, then another—three moons in two months—and not a single fire was kindled in the houses of the Messenger of Allah ﷺ." ʿUrwa said, "Dear aunt! How did you all survive?" ʿĀʾisha replied, "By the two black things: dates and water; however, the Messenger of Allah ﷺ had neighbors from the Helpers (*Anṣār*) and they owned some milch animals, and they would send him some of their milk to the Messenger of

301 Al-Tirmidhī, *Shamāʾil*.
302 Ibid.

Allah ﷺ and he would serve it to us."[303]

Abū Ṭalḥa ﷺ reported, "We complained of hunger to the Messenger of Allah ﷺ and lifted [the clothing] from our stomachs [to show him] the stones we had tied around them, and then he lifted [the clothing] from his stomach [and showed us] two stones tied around his."[304] Imam al-Tirmidhī commented, "This phrase, 'lifted [the clothing] from our stomachs [to show him] the stones we had tied around them,' means one of them would fasten a stone around his stomach due to intense strain and weakness caused by hunger."

In *al-Mawāhib* it is related that Ibn Bujayr ﷺ said, "One day the Prophet ﷺ experienced intense hunger and took a stone and fastened it around his stomach. Then he said, 'Ah, how many a well-fed and pleasure-filled soul in this world will be hungry and naked on the Day of Resurrection! Ah, how many a person who honors it is actually dishonoring it! Ah, how many a person who disdains his soul is actually honoring it!'"[305]

Abū Hurayra ﷺ reported, "The Messenger of Allah

303 Agreed upon.

304 Al-Tirmidhī, *Shamāʾil.*

305 The origin of this hadith is found in al-Mundhirī's *al-Targhīb wa al-tarhib* and al-Muttaqī al-Hindī's *Kanz al-ʿummāl.* The phrase "Ah, how many a person who honors it is actually dishonoring it!" means how many a person who seemingly honors it by giving it free rein to enjoy luxuries and desires is actually dishonoring it by distracting it from its ultimate purpose and preventing it from getting closer to Allah. The phrase "Ah, how many a person who disdains his soul is actually honoring it!" means how many a person who disdains his soul by opposing its appetites and desires is actually honoring it by making it ready for the Day of Resurrection and gaining lofty degrees in Paradise. See ʿAbdullāh b. Saʿid al-Laḥjī, *Muntahā al-sūl* (2:16). [t]

ﷺ came out one night at a late hour in which he would not usually come out, and at a time when he would not usually meet others. Abū Bakr came out to him and the Prophet asked, 'What brings you out, Abū Bakr?' Abū Bakr replied, 'I've come out to meet the Messenger of Allah ﷺ and gaze upon his face and greet him with the salutations of peace.' Moments later ʿUmar came out and the Prophet asked him, 'What brings you out, ʿUmar?' ʿUmar replied, 'Hunger, O Messenger of Allah!' The Messenger of Allah said, 'I too am experiencing some of that.'

"They then set out towards the house of Abū al-Haytham b. al-Tayyihān al-Anṣārī (he was a man who owned many date palm trees and sheep, but did not own a servant), but they did not find him [home], so they asked his wife, 'Where is your mate?' She replied, 'He went out to fetch some fresh water for us.'[306] A short while later Abū al-Haytham returned with a water-skin filled with water. He placed it down and went to embrace the Messenger of Allah ﷺ, and said 'May my father and mother be sacrificed for you!'

"Then he escorted them to his garden and laid out a spread for them and then went towards a date palm tree and returned with a branch that had a cluster of dates on it. He placed the cluster in front of them. The Messenger of Allah ﷺ said, 'Will you not pick out for us some of its fresh dates?' Abū al-Haytham said, 'O Messenger of Allah! I wished that you would pick from its ripe and unripe dates!' They began to eat and drink from that water. The Prophet ﷺ then said, 'By the One in Whose Hand is my soul, all of these—cool shade, fine ripe dates,

306 Because he did not have a servant to do it for him. [t]

and cold water—are from the bounties that you will be asked about on the Day of Resurrection'

"Abū al-Haytham then went out to prepare some food for them, and the Prophet ﷺ said, 'Do not slaughter for us a full grown sheep,' so he slaughtered for them a four month old she-goat or a goat that was not quite one years old. He brought it to them and they ate [of it]. The Prophet ﷺ asked him, 'Do you have a servant?' 'No,' replied Abū al-Haytham. 'When we receive some captives,' the Prophet ﷺ said, 'come to us.'

"[Some time later] two captives were brought to the Prophet ﷺ (and not a third), and Abū al-Haytham went to him. The Prophet ﷺ said, 'Pick from these two.' Abū al-Haytham said, 'Pick for me, O Messenger of Allah!' The Prophet ﷺ said, 'The one in whom counsel is sought is put in a position of trust (*muʾtaman*); take this one, for I have seen him praying. I bid you treat him well.'

"Abū al-Haytham then went to his wife and informed her of what the Messenger of Allah ﷺ had said. His wife replied, 'You will not be able to fulfill the right that the Prophet ﷺ instructed regarding him [the servant] unless you free him.' Abū al-Haytham said, 'In that case he is free.' The Messenger of Allah ﷺ said, 'Allah has not sent a Prophet or vicegerent except that he has two advisers: one adviser enjoining him to do good and forbidding him from evil, and another adviser that does not spare any effort to corrupt him. Verily, whoso is protected from an evil advisor is granted protection!'"[307]

Indeed, the protected person is the one who is protected by Allah Most High!

ʿUtba b. Ghazawān ﷺ said, "I saw myself, and I was

307 Al-Tirmidhī, *Shamāʾil*.

the seventh of seven people with the Messenger of Allah ﷺ. We had no food except for the leaves of trees that caused ulcers to flare around our mouths. I took a cloak and split it between myself and Saʿd [b. Mālik]. I covered myself with one half and Saʿd covered himself with the other half. There is none from among us except that he is now the leader of a city, and you will soon find that the rulers after us will not be like us!"[308]

Anas رضي الله عنه reported that the Messenger of Allah ﷺ said, "I was threatened with fear because of [calling to] Allah when no one but me was threatened with fear. I was harmed because of [calling to] Allah when no one else was harmed. Thirty consecutive days and nights would pass by and there was no food for Bilāl and I that was suitable for animals or humans, except for a miniscule portion of food that Bilāl kept hidden under his arm."[309] The compiler [Imam al-Tirmidhī] said in his *al-Jāmiʿ* [*al-ṣaḥīḥ*], "The meaning of this hadith is that the Prophet ﷺ was with Bilāl when he left from Mecca in escape, and Bilāl only had enough food that he could hide under his arm."

Anas رضي الله عنه said, "The Prophet ﷺ would not have bread and meat for lunch and dinner [on the same day] unless he had several guests."[310] [Al-Bājūrī said] "Thus the Prophet ﷺ did not have bread and meat for lunch and dinner unless he was entertaining guests[311], in which case

308 Ibid.

309 Ibid.

310 Ibid.

311 The word used in the hadith, *ḍafaf*, has also been defined as several guests who gather to eat a meal that is not large enough to cater to their numbers. This is an indication that the Prophet ﷺ would prefer to enjoy bread and meat in the company of others and not eat them alone. [t]

he would acquire both for their sake."

Nawfal b. Iyās al-Hudhalī said, "ʿAbd al-Raḥmān b. ʿAwf ﷺ used to host us, and what an excellent host he was! He walked with us [from the market] to his house one day until we entered his home. He went inside and bathed, and then came out and brought us a platter filled with bread and meat. When the platter was placed on the ground ʿAbd al-Raḥmān began to weep. I asked him, 'O ʿAbd al-Raḥmān! What causes you to weep?' He said, 'The Messenger of Allah ﷺ passed away and neither he nor his Household at their fill of barley bread—and I don't think that we have been caused to linger with what is better for us!'"[312]

Anas ﷺ reported that dates were brought to the Messenger of Allah ﷺ. [He said] "I saw him eating [them] while leaning back [upon something] out of hunger."[313]

[Imam al-Ghazālī said] "The Prophet ﷺ would not take of the things which Allah gave him save his provision of a year, and of that only the simplest foodstuffs he found, such as dates and barley, the rest of which he would give in charity for the sake of Allah."[314]

Al-Bukhārī and Muslim both narrated that the

312 Al-Tirmidhī, *Shamāʾil*. ʿAbd al-Raḥmān's somewhat obscure phrase "I don't think that we have been caused to linger with what is better for us!" means: If the Prophet's condition was such that he left this world having not eaten his fill of even barley bread and he is the best of creation, how can we consider our condition better, especially when luxury and opulence might be one's sole recompense in this life before returning to Allah empty-handed on the Day of Judgment. See ʿAbdullāh b. Saʿīd al-Laḥjī, *Muntahā al-sūl* (2:36).

313 Muslim, *Ṣaḥīḥ*.

314 Al-Ghazālī, *Iḥyāʾ ʿulūm al-dīn*.

Messenger of Allah ﷺ would set aside a year's worth of provision for his family.

ʿĀʾisha ﷺ said, "The Messenger of Allah ﷺ did not leave leftovers of lunch for dinner, or leftovers of dinner for lunch [the next day]."[315]

Al-Tirmidhī narrated from Anas ﷺ that the Messenger of Allah ﷺ never stored anything for the morrow.[316]

When the Messenger of Allah ﷺ would eat lunch he would not eat dinner [that evening], and if he ate dinner he would not eat lunch [the day after].[317]

Al-Qasṭalānī said in *al-Mawāhib al-laduniyya*:

> The lengthy days of hunger experienced by the Prophet ﷺ and his Companions have been deemed problematic in light of other narrations, such as:
>
> the narration of him ﷺ setting aside a year's worth of provision for his family;
> the narration of him ﷺ dividing one thousand camels taken as *fayʾ*[318] between four Companions;
>
> the narration of him bringing along one hundred camels on his journey for the ʿUmra, all of which he sacrificed and distributed to the poor;
>
> and the narration in which he ﷺ gave instructions for a Bedouin Arab to be given a large number of sheep, and many other narrations of this sort.

315 Because of his reliance upon Allah. [t]

316 Al-Tirmidhī, *al-Jāmiʿ*.

317 Recorded by Abū Nuʿaym in *Ḥilyat al-Awliyāʾ* with a weak chain of transmission. This narration means (assuming it is soundly reported) that the Prophet ﷺ would not eat twice in the day. [t]

318 Spoils captured without fighting. [t]

Furthermore, many of the Prophet's Companions were wealthy, such as Abū Bakr, ʿUmar, ʿUthmān, Ṭalḥa, and others, and they had spent freely from their wealth and lives for him. [In one narration] the Prophet ﷺ ordered the Companions to give in charity and Abū Bakr came with all of his wealth, and ʿUmar came with half of his. [And in another narration] the Prophet encouraged the Companions to equip the Army of Hardship (*Jaysh al-ʿUsra*), and ʿUthmān equipped them by providing one thousand camels.

This confusion has been answered by al-Ṭabarī (as quoted in *Fatḥ al-Bārī*[319]), who said that this [hunger] "was intermittent and not due to destitution or straightened means; rather, it was sometimes because they chose to prefer others over themselves, and other times it was out of dislike for satiety and eating too much food." Al-Ḥāfiẓ Ibn Ḥajar said, "The truth of the matter is that several of them were of straightened means whilst in Mecca before the migration, and then, when they [the Muslims] migrated to Medina, most of them were in that state. As a result, the Helpers lent them a helping hand by providing them homes and servants, and after they conquered [Banū] Naḍīr and secured other victories they gave the servants back. It is true that the Prophet ﷺ chose this way for himself and was able to secure luxury and ease for himself in this world—as al-Tirmidhī narrated from the hadith of Abū Umāma who reported that the Prophet ﷺ said,

319 The famous commentary on *Ṣaḥīḥ al-Bukhārī* written by Ibn Ḥajar al-ʿAsqalānī. [t]

'My Lord presented the mountains of Mecca to me and offered to turn them into gold and silver, but I said, "O Lord! I prefer to go hungry one day and eat to my fill the next: on the day in which I go hungry I turn fervently to You and call upon you, and on the day in which I eat to my fill I praise and extol You!"' And in another report, Ibn ʿAbbās ﷺ said, 'One day the Messenger of Allah ﷺ and Jibrīl were atop Ṣafā, and the Messenger of Allah ﷺ said, "O Jibrīl, by the One Who has sent you with the truth, the Household of Muḥammad does not pass the evening with even a handful of meal flour or porridge!" No sooner had he finished speaking than a booming sound came from the heavens, frightening him. The Messenger of Allah ﷺ said, 'Has Allah commanded for the resurrection to take place now?' Jibrīl replied, 'No, but when He heard your words He ordered Isrāfīl to descend to you.' Isrāfīl came to him and said, 'Verily Allah Most High has heard what you said; He has sent me with the Keys to the treasures of the earth and told me to offer them to you. If you like I can turn the mountains of Tihāma into rubies and emeralds, and gold and silver, or if you wish you can be a Prophet-king, and if you wish you can be a Prophet-servant.' Jibrīl signaled to him to prefer humility, so the Prophet said three times, 'Rather, a Prophet-servant.' This was narrated by al-Ṭabarānī with an authentic (*ḥasan*) chain of transmission."

How excellent are the words of al-Buṣīrī:

Lofty mountains sought to tempt him by
transforming to gold
But O what lofty height he showed them!

As for the bread of the Messenger of Allah ﷺ, Ibn ʿAbbās ﷺ said, "The Messenger of Allah ﷺ and his Family would spend consecutive nights famished and would not find anything to eat for dinner. The most common form of bread they would eat was barley bread."[320]

ʿĀʾisha ﷺ said, "The Family of Muḥammad ﷺ never ate their fill of barley bread two nights in a row until the Messenger of Allah ﷺ passed away."[321]

Sulaym b. ʿĀmir said, "I heard Abū Umāma [al-Bāhilī] ﷺ say, 'There was never any excess barley bread[322] left in the house of the Messenger of Allah ﷺ.'"[323]

ʿĀʾisha ﷺ said, "A chunk of bread was not eaten from the Prophet's spread ﷺ until he passed away."

ʿĀʾisha ﷺ is also reported to have said, "When the Messenger of Allah ﷺ passed away I had nothing fit to eat for an animal or human except half a *wasq*[324] of barley kept on a shelf of mine. I ate from it for a long time until finally I weighted it and it was soon used up."

The Messenger of Allah ﷺ would eat unsifted barley bread, and it would sometimes get stuck in his throat and could only be swallowed after taking a gulp of water.[325]

It is reported that Sahl b. Saʿd ﷺ was asked, "Did the Messenger of Allah ﷺ ever eat bread made from fine flour?" Sahl replied, "The Messenger of Allah ﷺ did not even see fine flour until he met Allah." Then he was asked, "During the time of the Messenger of Allah ﷺ did you

320 Al-Tirmidhī, *Shamāʾil.*

321 Ibid.

322 That is, there was never any leftover bread, and what bread they did have was usually not enough to sate them. [t]

323 Al-Tirmidhī, *Shamāʾil.*

324 Around 122 kilograms. [t]

325 Al-Ghazālī, *Iḥyāʾ ʿulūm al-dīn.*

have sieves?" Sahl replied, "We did not have sieves." Then he was asked, "So how did you make bread with barley?" Sahl replied, "We would blow into it and whatever large particles were in it would fly out, and then we would knead the rest into dough."[326] Another narration has it, "Did you have sieves during the time of the Messenger of Allah ﷺ?" Sahl replied, "The Prophet ﷺ never saw a sieve from the time Allah tasked him with the message until Allah took his soul."[327]

Anas ﷺ said, "I do not know of the Messenger of Allah ﷺ seeing a thin flat-bread until he met Allah—nor did he see a *samīṭ* styled lamb until he met Allah."[328] A *samīṭ* lamb is a lamb whose hair is removed by boiling water and then roasted with its skin intact. It is one of the practices of the people of opulence.

Qatāda related that Anas ﷺ said, "The Prophet of Allah ﷺ never ate upon a tray[329], or from a small plate[330], and never ate thin bread." Qatāda said, "They used to eat on round leather mats."[331]

Masrūq said, "One day I went to visit ʿĀʾisha ﷺ and she asked for some food to be brought to me. Then she said, 'I do not eat my fill of food and then wish to cry except that I cry.' I asked her, 'Why?' She replied, 'I remember the condition in which the Messenger of Allah ﷺ left this world; by Allah, he never ate his fill of

326 Al-Tirmidhī, *Shamāʾil*.
327 Ibid.
328 Al-Bukhārī, *Ṣaḥīḥ*.
329 A *khuwān*, a small table or tray at which one sits to eat. [t]
330 A *sukurruja*, a small plate or container that holds condiments like salad.
331 Al-Tirmidhī, *Shamāʾil*.

bread and meat twice in the same day!'"[332]

Abū Hurayra ؓ said, "The Family of Muḥammad ﷺ never ate their fill three days consecutively until his soul was taken."[333] Muslim narrated, "The Family of Muḥammad ﷺ never ate their fill of wheat bread two days in a row except that on one of the days it was mostly[334] dates."[335] Muslim also narrated from ʿĀʾisha ؓ, "The Messenger of Allah ﷺ passed away having never ate his fill of bread and oil twice in the same day!"[336] ʿĀʾisha ؓ also reported, "The Messenger of Allah ﷺ never ate his fill of barley bread in two consecutive days, though had he wanted, Allah would have given him what is unimaginable."

Al-Qasṭalānī said in *al-Mawāhib*:

> I have carefully searched through [the hadith literature] to find out if the flat-breads of the Prophet ﷺ were small or large, but after a thoroughgoing search I was unable to find anything. It is true, however, that it was narrated that he ordered flat-breads to be made small—there is, in a hadith on the authority of ʿĀʾisha ؓ (that is considered a raised (*marfūʿ*) narration from her to the Prophet ﷺ): "Make your breads small and increase their number, for then you will have blessings in them."
>
> My Shaykh, the lordly gnostic Ibrāhīm al-

332 Ibid.

333 Agreed upon.

334 That is, in one of the two days they ate mostly dates because of the small amount of bread available to them. [t]

335 Muslim, *Ṣaḥīḥ*.

336 Ibid.

> Matbūlī[337], used to have his flat-breads made small, and it was also the practice of Shaykh Abū al-ʿAbbās Aḥmad al-Badawī[338] and the esteemed masters of Banū Wafā[339]—may Allah Most High ever bestow on us from their blessings!

ʿĀʾisha ﷺ said, "He ﷺ left this world having not filled his belly with two foods together. If he ate his fill of dates he would not eat his fill of barley, and if he ate his fill of barley he would not eat his fill of dates."

Al-Qasṭalānī said:

> Know that satiety is the first innovation to arise after the first generation. Al-Nasāʾī and Ibn Mājah have narrated (and it authenticated by al-Ḥākim) from the hadith of al-Miqdām b. Maʿdī Karab that the Messenger of Allah ﷺ said, "The son of Ādam does not fill a vessel worse than his belly. It suffices the son of Ādam to eat a few morsels to keep his back upright. If the lower self of the son of Ādam

337 Shaykh Ibrāhīm al-Matbūlī (d. 877 AH) is one of the famous saints of Egypt and the spiritual teacher of Imam ʿAbd al-Wahhāb al-Shaʿrānī. A collection of his spiritual counsels is found in al-Shaʿrānī's two volume collection *al-Akhlāq al-Matbūliyya* (Cairo, Maktabat al-īmān, 2003)

338 Shaykh Aḥmad al-Badawī (d. 675 AH) is one of the most famous saints in all of Egypt. Originally from Fez, Morocco, al-Badawī settled in Egypt and was known for his spiritual charisma and miracles. He is buried in Tanta.

339 The "masters of Banū Wafā" refer to the scions of Shaykh Muḥammad Wafā (d. 769 AH), who were a highly respected family of spiritual masters from the descendants of Imam ʿAlī ﷺ and the trustees and caretakers of the Mosque and mausoleum of Imam al-Ḥusayn ﷺ.

overcomes him then let it be a third for food, a third for drink, and a third for breathing."

Al-Qurṭubī said, "Had Hippocrates heard of this division he would have been amazed with its wisdom."

Al-Ḥasan [al-Baṣrī] ﷺ said, "The Messenger of Allah ﷺ delivered a sermon and said, 'By Allah, the Family of Muḥammad—which consists of nine homes—does not enter the evening time with even a *ṣāʿ* of food.' By Allah, he did not say that to insinuate that Allah's provision was scanty, but rather he wanted his nation to emulate him."

In the *Shifā*, Qāḍī ʿIyāḍ said:

It is related that ʿĀʾisha ﷺ said, "The Prophet's belly was never full, and he never complained to anyone. Need was more beloved to him than wealth. He would at times be doubled over from hunger an entire night but that would not prevent him from fasting the next day. Had he wanted he could have asked his Lord for all the treasures and fruits of the world and a life of plenty. I used to weep out of pity for him, seeing him in such a state, and I would rub his belly with my hand because of his hunger. I would say, 'May my soul be ransom for you! If only you had enough of this world to feed you!' But he would reply, 'O ʿĀʾisha, what have I to do with this world? My brethren from the Messengers of High Resolve (*Ulū al-ʿAzm*) were patient with much worse than this. They were steadfast in their state and went on to their Lord, and He honored them in their return and gave them a bountiful reward;

therefore, I am too shy to enjoy a life of ease, lest tomorrow my station is less than theirs. There is nothing more beloved to me than joining my brethren and close friends.' It was not even a month after he said this that he passed away, may Allah send prayers and peace upon him!"

Then he [Qāḍī ʿIyāḍ] said some three pages later:

Dāwūd (may prayers and peace be upon him) used to wear woolen garments and sleep on a bedding of hair. He would eat barley bread with salt and ashes. He would mix his drink with tears.

ʿĪsā ﷺ was asked, "Why do you not take a donkey [to ride upon]?" He replied, "I am too noble in the sight of Allah to be distracted by a donkey!" He used to wear woolen garments and eat from trees. He did not have a home and would only sleep where sleep overcame him. The name he like to be called the most was "the poor one" (al-Miskīn).

It is said that when Mūsā [ﷺ] reached the water [well] of Midian he was so emaciated that the green color of onions could be seen from his stomach."[340] The Prophet ﷺ said, "Among the Prophets before me were some tested by poverty and lice, and that would be more beloved to them than receiving gifts would be to you."[341]

Mujāhid said, "Yaḥyā's food was herbage. He

340 That is, he was so hungry and emaciated when he arrived at the well of Midian that his stomach was virtually translucent and it was possible to see the green color of some onions he had eaten. [t]

341 Al-Ḥākim, *al-Mustadrak*.

would weep out of reverence for Allah Most High until his tears etched lines on his cheeks."

Al-Ṭabarī related on the authority of Wahb [b. Munabbih] that Mūsā (prayers and peace be upon him) used to take shade underneath a canopy and eat from a depression within a stone. Out of humility before Allah and on account of being honored with Divine Speech, when he wanted to drink he would lap from it like an animal laps water.

SECTION TWO

The Description of the Prophet's Manners of Eating & His Condiments ﷺ

KAʿB B. ʿUJRA ﷺ said, "I saw the Messenger of Allah ﷺ eating with his three fingers—with his thumb, his index finger, and his middle finger—and I then saw him lick [the utensil] with the same three fingers before wiping them clean."[342]

The Messenger of Allah ﷺ disliked eating very hot food until it simmered down.[343]

The Messenger of Allah ﷺ did not eat very hot food, regarding which he would say, "It is without blessing; Allah did not feed us fire, so make it cool."[344]

The Messenger of Allah ﷺ would eat from what was nearest to him. He would eat with three, occasionally four, fingers, but did not eat with two fingers, regarding which he ﷺ said, "That is the way Satan eats."[345]

The Messenger of Allah ﷺ would lick the plate clean with his fingers and say, "The last portion of food [in the

342 Al-Haythamī, *Majmaʿ al-zawāʾid*.
343 Al-Muttaqī al-Hindī, *Kanz al-ʿummāl*.
344 Al-ʿAjlūnī, *Kashf al-khafā*.
345 Al-Ṭabarānī, *al-Muʿjam al-kabīr*.

plate] contains the most blessings."[346]

He would lick his fingers free of food until they turned red, and would not wipe his hands with a cloth until he licked each finger individually. He would say, "It is not known in which portion of the food there contains blessings."[347]

When the Prophet would eat bread and meat especially, he would wash his hands vigorously and wipe his face with the excess water.[348]

Ibn ʿUmar reported, "The Messenger of Allah said, 'Whoso eats anything of this meat should wash his hands to remove its smell and stain and not offend the person next to him.'"[349]

When he sat to eat, the Prophet would most often join his knees and feet together as one praying sits down; however, one knee would be over the other knee, and one foot over the other foot. He would say, "I am but a servant; I eat as a servant eats, and sit as a servant sits."[350]

Abū Juḥayfa reported, "The Messenger of Allah said, 'As for me, I do not eat while reclining.'" And Ibn Mājah narrated that the Messenger of Allah forbade that one eat while lying on his stomach.[351] Ibn ʿAdī recorded that the Messenger of Allah forbade that one eat while leaning on his left hand.[352]

346 Al-Zabīdī, *Itḥāf al-sādat al-muttaqīn.*
347 Aḥmad, *Musnad.*
348 Al-Zabīdī, *Itḥāf al-sādat al-muttaqīn.*
349 Ibid.
350 Ibid.
351 Ibn Mājah, *Sunan.*
352 Ibn ʿAdī, *al-Kāmil fī al-ḍuʿafāʾ.*

As for the condiments of the Messenger of Allah ﷺ, he did not avoid or shun any lawful food. If he found dates instead of bread he would eat of them; if he found roasted meat he would eat of it; if he found wheat bread he would eat of it; if he found barley bread he would eat of it; if he found sweets he would eat of them; if he found honey he would eat of it; if he found milk instead of bread he would drink of it and suffice himself with it; and if he found watermelon or fresh dates he would eat of them.

The Messenger of Allah ﷺ would eat what was present and never refuse what was available. Zahdam al-Jarmī said, "We were once in the company of Abū Mūsā al-Ashʿarī ؓ when some chicken meat was brought for us to eat. A man distanced himself from the group and Abū Mūsā said, 'What is the matter with you?' The man replied, 'I saw the chicken eating something unclean so I swore that I would not eat it.' Abū Mūsā said, 'Come, for I saw the Messenger of Allah ﷺ eat chicken meat.'"[353]

Ibrāhīm b. ʿUmar b. Safīna related on the authority of his father who related on the authority of his grandfather Safīna, the freed bondsman of the Messenger of Allah ﷺ, who said, "I ate the meat of a houbara bustard with the Messenger of Allah ﷺ."[354] (The houbara bustard is a fowl with a long neck and beak, and it is ash-colored and an agile flyer.)

The Prophet ﷺ used to eat hunted fowl, but did not follow the hunt or hunt it himself. Instead, he preferred that it be hunted for him and brought to him, of which he would eat.[355]

The Prophet ﷺ would say to ʿĀʾisha ؓ, "When you

353 Al-Tirmidhī, *Shamāʾil*.

354 Ibid.

355 Al-Zabīdī, *Itḥāf al-sādat al-muttaqīn*.

cook a pot of food, be sure put in it many gourds, for gourds help strengthen the heart of one aggrieved.'"[356]

The Prophet ﷺ would [also] eat *tharīd* with meat and pumpkin.[357] He ﷺ loved pumpkins and said concerning them, "It is the tree of my brother Yūnus ﷺ."[358]

Jābir b. Ṭāriq ﷺ said, "I went to see the Prophet ﷺ and saw a gourd being sliced. I asked, 'What is that for?' and he said, 'We increase our food with it.'"[359]

Anas ﷺ said, "A tailor once invited the Messenger of Allah ﷺ for a meal he had prepared." I went with the Messenger of Allah to partake of that food. He was presented with barley bread and a broth that had pieces of gourd and dried strips of meat in it. I saw the Messenger of Allah ﷺ seek out the pieces of gourd from the sides of the bowl. From that day forward I have not ceased loving gourd!"[360] Al-Nawawī said, "This indicates that it is recommended for a person to love gourd, and likewise everything that the Prophet ﷺ loved."[361]

ʿĀʾisha ﷺ said, "The Prophet ﷺ loved sweet foods[362] and honey."[363]

The most beloved of drinks to the Messenger of Allah ﷺ was water infused with honey.[364]

The most beloved of drinks[365] to the Messenger of Allah

356 Ibid.

357 Ibn Ḥajar, *al-Maṭālib al-ʿāliya*.

358 Ibn Ḥajar, *Fatḥ al-Bārī*.

359 Al-Tirmidhī, *Shamāʾil*.

360 Ibid.

361 Al-Nawawī, *Sharḥ Ṣaḥīḥ Muslim*.

362 The meaning of sweet foods here are all types of sweets, whether manmade or natural, including fruits. [t]

363 Al-Tirmidhī, *Shamāʾil*.

364 Al-Dhahabī, *al-Ṭibb al-Nabawī*.

365 The apparent contradiction between this narration and the

ﷺ was milk.[366] When he would drink milk, he would say "It contains fat." The Messenger of Allah ﷺ would occasionally drink pure milk and occasionally drink it mixed with cool water. When milk would be brought to him, the Prophet ﷺ would say, "It is a blessing."[367] The Prophet ﷺ would sometimes combine between dates and milk and call them "the two fine things."

The Prophet ﷺ would eat dates with butter, and liked it. In the *Iḥyāʾ* [*ʿulūm al-dīn*] it mentions that ʿUthmān b. ʿAffān brought the Prophet ﷺ some *fālūdhaj* [a sweet made of flour and honey] and he ate of it. The Prophet ﷺ asked, "What is this, O ʿAbdullāh?" ʿUthmān said, "May my father and mother be sacrificed for you! We take some clarified butter and honey and put it in a stone cooking pot, put it over a fire and boil it. Then we take the choice kernels of wheat when it is milled, and roast it over the clarified butter and honey in the pot. We then mix it until it is fully cooked, and the result is what you see." The Messenger of Allah ﷺ said, "This food is good." (This incident was mentioned in *al-Mawāhib* [*al-laduniyya*] on the authority of ʿAbdullāh b. Salām with a slightly different rendering. In it, it says that the Prophet called this food *khabīṣ*.)

The most beloved food to the Prophet ﷺ was meat, of which he would say, "It strengthens hearing and is the master of all foods in this life and the Next. Had I asked my Lord to feed it to me every day He would have done so."

one preceding it was reconciled by some scholars, who said that milk is superior for nourishment and food while honey is superior in a general sense. [t]

366 Al-Muttaqī al-Hindī, *Kanz al-ʿummāl*.

367 Ibid.

ʿAṭāʾ b. Yasār related that Umm Salama ﷺ informed him that she presented the Messenger of Allah ﷺ with a roasted side portion of meat, of which he ate.[368] ʿAbdullāh b. al-Ḥārith said, "We ate a roasted lamb with the Messenger of Allah ﷺ while in the Mosque."[369] Al-Mughīra b. Shuʿba ﷺ said, "I was with the Messenger of Allah ﷺ one night as a guest. A roasted side of meat was presented to him and he took a large knife and he began to slice it—and he sliced a piece for me. Bilāl came and informed the Prophet ﷺ that it was the time of prayer. The Prophet placed the knife down and said, 'What is with him? May his hands be dusty!'[370] Bilāl's mustache had grown long so he [the Prophet ﷺ] said to him, 'I shall trim it for you by placing a tooth-stick (*siwāk*) on your upper lip'—or he said 'You must trim it by placing a tooth-stick (*siwāk*) on your upper lip.'"[371]

The Prophet ﷺ would eat liver if it was roasted, and he liked the foreshank and shoulder of lamb.

Abū Hurayra ﷺ reported, "The Prophet ﷺ was brought some meat and presented with the foreshank, and he bit into it."[372]

Ibn Masʿūd ﷺ reported, "The Prophet ﷺ liked the foreshank. It was a foreshank that was poisoned, and it was thought that the Jews had poisoned him."[373]

Abū ʿUbayda ﷺ said, "I cooked a pot of stew[374]

368 Al-Tirmidhī, *Shamāʾil*.

369 Ibid.

370 The Prophet ﷺ said this because it is offensive to offer prayer once food has been served. [t]

371 Al-Tirmidhī, *Shamāʾil*.

372 Ibid.

373 Ibid.

374 With sheep. [t]

for the Prophet, and he liked the foreshank, so I gave him a foreshank from it. Then he said, 'Pass me its foreshank,' so I passed it to him. Then he said, 'Pass me its foreshank.' I said to him, 'O Messenger of Allah! How many foreshanks does a sheep have?' He replied, 'By Him in Whose Hand is my soul, if only you had been silent, you would have given me as many foreshanks as I asked for!'"[375]

ʿĀʾisha ﷺ said, "The foreshank was the most beloved portion of meat to the Messenger of Allah ﷺ; however, he would only find meat to eat occasionally, and he would take to it [the foreshank] quickly because it was the quickest portion to cook."[376]

The most beloved portion of sheep to the Messenger of Allah ﷺ was the forsaddle.[377]

ʿAbdullāh b. Jaʿfar ﷺ said, "I heard the Messenger of Allah ﷺ say, 'The choicest cut of meat is the back.'"[378]

Ḍubāʿa b. al-Zubayr ﷺ reported that she slaughtered a sheep at her house and the Messenger of Allah ﷺ sent a message to them [her family] saying "Give us to eat from your sheep." She said, "All we had left was its neck, and I was ashamed to send it to the Prophet ﷺ." [The messenger] went back and informed the Messenger of Allah ﷺ of what she said. He replied, "Go back and tell her to send it, for it is the easiest part of the sheep [to digest], and the

375 Al-Tirmidhī, *Shamāʾil*.

376 Ibid.

377 That is, the front cuts such as the foreshank, neck, shoulder, ribs, and loins. The commentators say this was because the front-saddle portions are easier to digest and further away from areas of impurity. [t]

378 Al-Tirmidhī, *Shamāʾil*.

closest of it to good and furthest[379] of it from harm."[380]

When the Messenger of Allah ﷺ would eat meat he would not lower his head towards it; rather, he would raise it up to his mouth and bite it.

The Messenger of Allah ﷺ ate cured meat[381]—this was recorded in the *Sunan* collections on the authority of a man[382] who said, "I slaughtered a sheep for the Messenger of Allah ﷺ while we were on a journey and he said, 'Preserve its meat.'[383] I continued to give him of this meat until we arrived in Medina."[384]

The Messenger of Allah ﷺ ate wild ass (*al-ḥimār al-waḥshī*)[385] and mutton. He also ate camel meat when travelling and resident.[386] He ﷺ also ate rabbit meat[387] and seafood.[388]

The Prophet ﷺ would eat *tharīd,* which is a dish prepared by mixing pieces of bread in a meat broth, and can also be prepared with meat. It is said as a figure of speech among the Arabs "*Tharīd* is one of the two meats."

The Prophet ﷺ would eat bread with oil. ʿUmar b. al-Khaṭṭāb ﷺ reported that the Messenger of Allah ﷺ said, "Eat olive oil and apply its oil [on you], for it comes from a blessed tree."[389]

379 That is, it is the easiest portion to digest and the furthest from the sexual organs. [t]
380 Aḥmad, *Musnad.*
381 *Qadīd,* or strips of meat that are dried in the sun. [t]
382 From the Companions. [t]
383 That is, dry it out and cure it so it does not spoil. [t]
384 Al-Ḥākim, *al-Mustadrak.*
385 Agreed upon.
386 Al-Nasāʾī, *Sunan.*
387 Agreed upon.
388 Muslim, *Ṣaḥīḥ.*
389 Al-Tirmidhī, *Shamāʾil.*

The Prophet ﷺ ate chard cooked with barely.[390]

The Prophet ﷺ ate *khazīra,* which is a barley cake in the shape of ʿ*aṣida*[391], only smaller.[392]

The Prophet ﷺ ate *uqṭ,* which is cheese made from milk curdling (and most closely resembles bulgur).

The Prophet ﷺ ate ripened dates (*ruṭab*), dry dates (*tamar*), and green dates (*busr*). He also ate *kabāth*[393], which is a fruit that grows on the arak tree.[394]

The Prophet ﷺ would eat cheese. Ibn ʿUmar ﷺ reported, "The Prophet ﷺ was brought some cheese while at Tabūk. He asked for a knife, pronounced [Allah's] name over it, and cut it."[395]

As for onions, Abū Dāwūd narrated in his *Sunan* on the authority of ʿĀʾisha ﷺ who, when asked about onions, said, "The last dish eaten by the Messenger of Allah contained onions."[396] What is apparent is that these onions were cooked so that no foul odor remained; this is proven by ʿĀʾisha's statement "contained onions," since she did not say "he ate onions."

Of seasonings, the Messenger of Allah preferred vinegar. ʿĀʾisha ﷺ reported that the Prophet ﷺ said, "What an excellent condiment vinegar is!"[397] Ibn ʿAbbās

390 Al-Tirmidhī, *al-Jāmiʿ*.

391 *Khazīra* is made by cutting meat into small pieces and pouring water on them and grinding them up and mixing them with flour and clarified butter. If there is no meat inside the dish is called ʿ*aṣida*. [t]

392 Al-Bukhārī, *Ṣaḥīḥ*.

393 Muslim, *Ṣaḥīḥ*.

394 The same tree whose roots and branches provide the *siwāk* tooth-stick recommended by the Prophet ﷺ. [t]

395 Abū Dāwūd, *Sunan*.

396 Ibid.

397 Al-Tirmidhī, *Shamāʾil*.

ﷺ reported, "On the day of the Conquest of Mecca the Messenger of Allah ﷺ went to see Umm Hāniʾ ﷺ. He was hungry. He asked her, 'Do you have any food to eat?' Umm Hāniʾ replied, 'No, except for some dry bread, but I am too ashamed to present it to you.' He said, 'Bring it,' and thereafter began breaking it and soaking it in water. She then brought him some salt, and he asked 'Is there any condiment?' She replied, 'I have nothing except a bit of vinegar.' He said, 'Bring it.' When she brought it, the Prophet ﷺ poured it over his food and ate, then he praised Allah and lauded Him, and then said, 'What an excellent condiment vinegar is, Umm Hāniʾ, for indeed no home that has vinegar is bereft.'"[398]

Umm Saʿd ﷺ said, "The Messenger of Allah ﷺ entered to see ʿĀʾisha while I was in her company. He asked, 'Is there any lunch?' She replied, 'We have some bread, dates, and vinegar.' He said, 'What an excellent condiment vinegar is—O Allah, bless vinegar, for indeed it was the condiment of the Prophets before me, and no home containing it will be bereft.'"[399]

This praise of vinegar, as Ibn al-Qayyim said, was circumstantial and not an absolute preference for it over other foods; it was to comfort and gratify the one who presented it to him ﷺ and not a preference for it over other foods; had he been presented with meat or honey or milk they would have had more right to praise. Thus it is understood that there is no contradiction between this [statement in praise of vinegar] and his statement "What a horrible condiment vinegar is!"[400]

398 Al-Bayhaqī, *Shuʿab al-īmān*.
399 Ibn Mājah, *Sunan*.
400 Al-ʿAjlūnī said in *Kashf al-khafā*, "This is a baseless narration (*lā aṣl lahu*)." [t]

Abū Mūsā al-Ashʿarī ﷺ reported that the Prophet ﷺ said, "The virtue of ʿĀʾisha over your women is like the virtue of *tharīd* over other foods."[401]

Anas b. Mālik ﷺ said, "On the occasion of the marriage celebration with Ṣafiyya, the Messenger of Allah fed [the guests] with dates and *sawīq*."[402] *Sawīq* is made from wheat or barley.

Salmā, the wife of Abū Rāfiʿ the freed bondsman of the Prophet ﷺ, reported that al-Ḥasan b. ʿAlī, Ibn ʿAbbās, and Ibn Jaʿfar came to her and said, "Prepare some food for us which the Messenger of Allah liked and enjoyed eating." She said, "Dear sons, you will not enjoy it today." They said, "Of course we will; prepare some for us." She stood up and gathered some barley, grounded it up, and put it inside a pot, then she poured some oil over it and grounded some pepper and *tawābil* and added them to the mix. Then she presented the dish to them and said, "This is what Prophet ﷺ liked and enjoyed eating."[403] *Tawābil* are spicy chilies from India. It is also said that it is a spice mixture of coriander, ginger, and cumin. [Al-Bājūrī said:] "It is adduced from this narration that the Prophet ﷺ liked to season food to make it more palatable—doing so with what was easy and available—and that it does not contradict non-attachment to the world (*zuhd*)."

Jābir b. ʿAbdullāh ﷺ said, "When the trench was being dug [before the Battle of the Confederates] I saw the Messenger of Allah ﷺ in a state of intense hunger. I went to my wife and asked, 'Do you have anything to eat? I saw the Messenger of Allah in a state of intense hunger!'

401 Al-Tirmidhī, *Shamāʾil*.
402 Ibid.
403 Ibid.

She brought out a bag containing a *ṣāʿ*[404] of barley. We also had small house-lamb.[405] I slaughtered it while she grounded up the barley into flour. Finally, when we were done, we put the meat into an earthenware pot and I went back to the Messenger of Allah and whispered to him what we had done and said, 'Come, you and a small group with you.' Immediately the Messenger of Allah shouted, 'O People of the Ditch! Jābir has prepared a feast for you, so come along!' Then he ﷺ said, 'Do not remove your pot from the hearth or bake the bread until I arrive.'

"When the Prophet arrived she brought out the kneaded flour and then he spat in it and blessed it, then he went over to our earthenware pot and spat inside of it and blessed it, too. Then he said, 'Call another baker who can bake bread with you, and ladle the soup from your earthenware pot, but do not remove it from the hearth.' Now, the guests were a thousand, and I swear by Allah that all of them ate [to their fill] until they left the meal and went away, and our earthenware pot was still boiling as it was before—brimming and full—and there was still kneaded dough [uncooked]."[406]

Jābir also reported, "I accompanied the Messenger of Allah ﷺ as he went to see a woman from the Helpers. She had slaughtered a sheep for him and he ate from it. She then brought him a plate of fresh dates and he ate from it. Then he performed ablutions for the Noon Prayer (Ẓuhr) and offered the prayer. Then, after he finished the prayer, she brought him what was left over

404 2.3 Liters. [t]

405 Literally, a small lamb left to roam in the house and not left to graze. [t]

406 Agreed upon.

from the sheep and he ate from it. Then he prayed the Late Noon Prayer (ʿAṣr) and did not perform [fresh] ablutions."[407]

Umm al-Mundhir[408] ﷺ said, "The Messenger of Allah once came to see me and ʿAlī was accompanying him. We had some suspended dates.[409] The Messenger of Allah ﷺ began to eat from them, as did ʿĀlī with him. He then said to ʿAlī, 'Enough, ʿAlī, for you have just recovered from an illness,' so ʿAlī sat down and the Messenger of Allah continued to eat. I prepared for them some chard and barley and the Messenger of Allah ﷺ said to ʿAlī, 'Take from this, for it is more suitable for you.'"[410]

ʿAbdullāh b. Salām ﷺ said, "I saw the Prophet ﷺ take a piece of barley bread, place a date on it, and say, 'This [the date] is a condiment for this [the barley bread].'"[411]

Anas ﷺ said, "The Messenger of Allah ﷺ liked *thufl*."[412] *Thufl* is the left-over food that is at the bottom of a pot, dish, or plate and the like.

The most beloved food to the Messenger of Allah ﷺ was *tharīd* made of bread or *tharīd* made of *ḥays*.[413] *Ḥays* is made of dates along with clarified butter and milk curdling, and is sometimes used to replace *uqṭ* or crumbled bread. All of them are mixed together [and made into *tharīd*].

Of cuts of sheep the Messenger of Allah ﷺ liked the

407 Al-Tirmidhī, *Shamāʾil*.
408 Salmā b. Qays, one of the aunts of the Prophet ﷺ. [t]
409 "Suspended dates" are green dates left hanging on the stalk and are eaten bit by bit as they ripen. [t]
410 Al-Tirmidhī, *Shamāʾil*.
411 Ibid.
412 Ibid.
413 Abū Dāwūd, *Sunan*.

foreshank and shoulder; of stews he liked gourds; of seasonings he liked vinegar; and of dates he liked the ʿ*ajwa* dates [native to Medina]. He called ʿ*ajwa* dates blessed and said, "It is of the Garden and is a remedy for poison and sorcery."

The most beloved of dates to the Messenger of Allah ﷺ were ʿ*ajwa* dates.

The Prophet ﷺ loved to eat butter and dates together.

Of vegetables, the Prophet ﷺ liked endive[414], mountain balm[415], and purslane.[416]

The Prophet ﷺ loved cucumberʾ[417] and palm pith.[418]

The Prophet ﷺ disliked eating kidneys on account of their proximity to urine. There were seven parts of sheep that he disliked and would not eat: the male organ, the ovaries, the bladder, the gall bladder, the thyroid gland, the vulva, and blood—and it is considered offensive for others to eat of them.[419]

The Prophet ﷺ did not eat locusts or kidneys.[420]

The Prophet ﷺ also found lizard[421] and spleen[422] distasteful but did not declare them unlawful.

Because the angels would come to him and Jibrīl would speak to him, the Prophet ﷺ did not eat garlic, onions, or leeks.

414 Cichorium endivia.
415 Eriodictyon californicum.
416 Portulaca oleracea.
417 Al-Haythamī, *Majmaʿ al-zawāʾid.*
418 Palm pith is an edible tuber that grows on the upper end of a date-palm trunk. [t]
419 Al-Ṭabarānī, *al-Muʿjam al-awsaṭ.*
420 Ibn Ṣarṣarī, *al-Amālī.*
421 Agreed upon.
422 Ibn Mājah, Sunan

The Prophet ﷺ never found fault with food; if he liked a food he would eat of it, and if he disliked it he would leave it.

ʿĀʾisha ﷺ said, "The Prophet ﷺ would come to me and ask, 'Do you have anything to eat?' I would reply 'No,' to which he would say, 'I am fasting.' One day he came to me and I said to him, 'O Messenger of Allah, we were given a gift.' He asked, 'What is it?' I said, 'It is some *ḥays*.' He said, 'I woke up fasting,' then he ate."[423]

When food would be presented to the Messenger of Allah ﷺ he would ask, "Is it a gift or is it charity?" If it was charity he would say to his Companions, "Eat it" and he would not partake of it, but if it was a gift he would reach out with his hand and eat with them."[424]

Because of the incident with the poisoned sheep, the Prophet ﷺ would not eat from a gift until he had the giver eat from it first.

The Prophet ﷺ owned a young male camel and a ewe whose milk he and his family would drink. He disliked owning more than a hundred of livestock, and when he would exceed a hundred he would sacrifice the extra animals.

The Prophet ﷺ had some neighbors who owned milch animals. They would send him some of their meat and milk and he would eat and drink from them.[425]

The Prophet ﷺ owned seven she-goats used for milch. They were grazed by Umm Ayman, the Prophet's wet-nurse.

The Prophet ﷺ would go often to the orchards owned by his Companions and eat and gather firewood.

423 Al-Tirmidhī, *Shamāʾil*.
424 Muslim, *Ṣaḥīḥ*.
425 Agreed upon.

The Prophet ﷺ would respond to the invitation of freeman and slave alike. He would accept gifts even if they were just a gulp of milk or a rabbit thigh, and would give something in return. He would eat from gifts and not from charity.

When the Prophet ﷺ would be invited for a meal and others followed him he would inform the host and say, "This person followed us, so if you wish he can go back."

The Messenger of Allah ﷺ would not eat alone.

The most beloved food to the Messenger of Allah ﷺ was that upon which many hands would gather.

The Prophet ﷺ would tell his guest repeatedly to eat and would offer food to them repeatedly.

ʿĀʾisha said (and it was also related by her parents), "The Prophet's belly ﷺ was never filled to satiety. When he was among his family he would never ask them for food or express desire for it. If they fed him he would eat, and if they did not feed him he would accept it. They never fetched drink for him."

The Prophet ﷺ would occasionally go and get something to eat or drink on his own.

Salmān said, "I read in the Torah that the blessings of food are gained through ablutions done after eating. I mentioned that to the Prophet ﷺ and informed him of what I had read in the Torah. The Messenger of Allah ﷺ said, 'The blessings of food are gained through ablutions done before and after eating.'"[426] (What is meant by ablutions here are ablutions in a linguistic sense, i.e., to wash the hands.)

426 Al-Tirmidhī, *Shamāʾil*.

SECTION THREE

What the Prophet ﷺ Would Say Before & After Eating

WHEN A SPREAD of food[427] would be placed down, the Messenger of Allah ﷺ would say, "In the name of Allah. O Allah, make this [meal] a blessing that is thanked and one that leads to the blessing of the Garden."[428] When food would be presented to him he would say "In the name of Allah," and when he would finish he would say "O Allah, You have fed and given drink, You have freed from need and You have pleased, and You have guided and chosen, so to You is all praise for what You have given."[429] When the spread of food would be removed he would say "All praise is due to Allah—an abundant and pure praise. All praise is due to Allah who sufficed us and sheltered us, and whose blessings cannot be compensated, left, or dispensed with." [430]

When he would finish his meal, the Prophet ﷺ would say "O Allah, to You is all praise [for favors] that cannot

427 A *māʾida,* which can be a spread of food placed on the ground or a covering on a table. [t]
428 Al-ʿIrāqī, *al-Mughnī ʿan ḥaml al-asfār fī al-asfār.*
429 Aḥmad, *Musnad.*
430 Ibn al-Sunnī, *ʿAmal al-yawm wa al-layla.*

be denied, compensated, or dispensed with."[431]

Abū Saʿīd al-Khudrī ﷺ said, "When the Messenger of Allah ﷺ would finish his meal he would say, 'All praise is due to Allah who has fed us, provided us drink, and made us Muslims.'"[432]

When the Messenger of Allah ﷺ would eat or drink he would say, "All praise is due to Allah who fed and provided drink, and made it easy to swallow, and provided a way out for it."[433]

Abū Ayyūb al-Anṣārī ﷺ said, "We were with the Prophet ﷺ one day and food was presented to him. I had never seen any food with more blessings when we began eating it and fewer blessings when we finished eating it. We said, 'O Messenger of Allah! How can this be?' He said, 'We mentioned Allah's name when we began to eat, and then someone sat to partake of the food but did not mention Allah's name, and so Satan ate with him.'"[434]

ʿĀʾisha ﷺ said, "One day, as the Prophet ﷺ was eating along with six of his Companions, a Bedouin joined them and finished the food in two [large] bites. The Messenger of Allah then said, 'Had he mentioned [Allah's] name it would have sufficed you all.'"[435] ʿĀʾisha ﷺ also reported that the Messenger of Allah ﷺ said, "When one of you eats and forgets to mention Allah's name over his food, let him say 'In the name of Allah in its beginning and end.'"[436]

431 Al-Haythamī, *Majmaʿ al-zawāʾid.*
432 Al-Tirmidhī, *Shamāʾil.*
433 Ibn Abī al-Dunyā, *Kitāb al-shukr.*
434 Al-Tirmidhī, *Shamāʾil.*
435 Ibid.
436 Ibid.

When the Messenger of Allah ﷺ would eat with a people, he would not leave until he supplicated for them. He would say, "O Allah, bless them and have mercy upon them." He would also say, "May those who are fasting break their fast with you, may the pious eat your food, and may the angels invoke prayers upon you."[437]

When the Messenger of Allah ﷺ would eat with a people he would be the last to eat.[438] It is reported that the Prophet ﷺ said, "When the food-spread is placed down one[439] should not get up, even if he is full, until the others are full as well, for doing so unsettles[440] those sitting and perhaps one of them is in need of food."[441]

ʿUmar b. Abī Salama, the stepson of the Messenger of Allah ﷺ, reported that he went to the Messenger of Allah ﷺ, who had some food with him. The Messenger of Allah ﷺ said to him, "Come close, dear son; mention Allah's name, eat with your right hand, and eat from what is nearest to you."[442]

ʿĀʾisha ﷺ said, "When food would be brought to the Messenger of Allah ﷺ he would eat from what was nearest to him, and when dates would be brought to him his hand would roam[443] [around the plate]."[444]

437 Ibn Abī Shayba, *Muṣannaf*.
438 Al-Tibrīzī, *Mishkāt al-maṣābīḥ*.
439 Meaning the host or one of the guests. [t]
440 Because if he gets up and leaves someone sitting and eating, the one sitting might fear being seen as greedy for food. [t]
441 Ibn Mājah, *Sunan*.
442 Al-Tirmidhī, *Shamāʾil*.
443 That is, when dates were presented to him ﷺ his hand would move around the plate picking whichever date he wanted, and he did not restrict himself to what was nearest to him. [t]
444 Abū al-Shaykh, *Akhlāq al-Nubuwwa*.

Anas ؓ reported that the Messenger of Allah ﷺ said, "Allah is pleased with the servant who, when he eats, praises Allah for it, and when he drinks, praises Allah for it."[445]

445 Al-Tirmidhī, *Shamāʾil.*

SECTION FOUR

The Description of the Prophet's Fruits ﷺ

THE MESSENGER OF Allah ﷺ would take fresh dates with his right hand and hold a melon in his left hand. He would eat fresh dates with melon, the latter being the most beloved fruit to him.[446]

The Messenger of Allah ﷺ would eat fresh dates and place their pits in a plate.[447]

The Messenger of Allah ﷺ would eat melon alongside fresh dates, and would say, "The heat of this cools that, and the coolness of that heats this.[448]

The Messenger of Allah ﷺ would eat melon alongside bread and sukkary [dates][449], or sometimes alongside

446 Al-Ḥākim, *al-Mustadrak*.

447 Ibid. Al-Munāwī notes that this plate would have been a small dish used exclusively for collecting date pits, since another hadith declares it offensive to place date pits in a plate of fresh dates. [t]

448 Al-Bayhaqī, *al-Sunan al-kubrā*.

449 *Sukkar* can also be translated as sugar; however, al-Ḥāfiẓ al-ʿIrāqī and Ibn Ḥajar al-Haytamī note that there is not a single authentic hadith stating that the Prophet ﷺ saw, much less ate, sugar, so the most likely interpretation of this hadith is that *sukkar* refers to the sukkary variety of dates, which are known for their sweetness. [t]

fresh dates, and would perhaps use two hands.

One day, as the Prophet ﷺ was eating fresh dates with his right hand and holding the date stones in his left hand, a sheep passed by, whereupon he showed her the date stones, and the sheep began eating out of his left hand while he ate with his right hand, until, when he was finished, the sheep left.[450]

Anas ﷺ said, "I saw the Messenger of Allah ﷺ combine yellow melon with fresh dates."[451]

The Messenger of Allah ﷺ would eat cucumber with fresh dates.[452] ʿĀʾisha ﷺ said, "My mother wanted me to put on some weight so she could present me[453] to the Messenger of Allah ﷺ but nothing worked for her until I began eating fresh dates with cucumber, which put weight on me in the best way." (This was narrated by Ibn Mājah. It was also narrated by al-Nasāʾī, but with "dates" in place of "fresh dates".)

The Messenger of Allah ﷺ would eat cucumber with fresh dates and salt. His favorite fresh fruit was melon and grape. He would sometimes eat grapes by putting the bunch in his mouth and drawing out its stalk bare; and in doing this the drops of water [from the grapes] would glisten on his beard, appearing like pearls.[454]

450 Al-Ḥāfiẓ al-ʿIrāqī said, "I have narrated this story in my collection *Fawāʾid Abī Bakr al-Shāfiʿī*, from the hadith of Anas with a weak chain." (*al-Mugnī ʿan ḥaml al-asfār ilā al-asfār*)

451 Al-Tirmidhī, *Shamāʾil.*

452 Ibid.

453 That is, in order to move in with him after their marriage. [t]

454 Al-Ḥāfiẓ al-ʿIrāqī, *al-Mugnī ʿan ḥaml al-asfār fī al-asfār* (declared extremely weak).

Al-Rubayyiʿ b. al-Muʿawwidh b. ʿAfrāʾ said, "Muʿādh[455] sent me with a tray full of fresh dates with small cucumber piled on top. The Prophet loved cucumber, so I brought it to him. He had some jewelry that was presented to him from Bahrain. He took a handful and gave it to me."[456]

When the Messenger of Allah would be presented with freshly harvested fruits he would place them over his eyes and lips and then say, "O Allah, just as You have shown the first of the harvest, show us the last." Then he would give the fruits to the children present with him.[457]

Abū Hurayra said, "When people would see the new fruits they would bring them to the Messenger of Allah. When the Messenger of Allah would take the fruit he would supplicate, 'O Allah! Bless our fruit, bless our Medina, and bless our *ṣāʿ* and our *mudd*.[458] O Allah! Verily Ibrāhīm is Your servant and Your intimate friend (*khalīl*) and Your Prophet—and I am Your servant and Your Prophet. He supplicated to You for Mecca, and I supplicate to You for Medina with the likes of which he supplicated to You regarding Mecca, and the likes thereof along with it.' Then he would call for the youngest child he saw and give him of that fruit."[459] The scholars note that the supplication of the Khalīl [Ibrāhīm] for Mecca was answered and that the supplication of the Beloved [Prophet Muḥammad] for Medina was answered, too, and thus fruits of every type have come to the two cities from the east and the west.

455 Muʿādh b. ʿAfrāʾ, her uncle. [t]
456 Al-Tirmidhī, *Shamāʾil*.
457 Al-Muttaqī al-Hindī, *Kanz al-ʿummāl*.
458 A *ṣāʿ* is 2.03 liters and a *mudd* is 0.51 liters. [t]
459 Al-Tirmidhī, *Shamāʾil*.

The Prophet would eat from the fruits of his land when available and in season and would not abstain from them. Al-Qasṭalānī said:

> This is one of the greatest means of good health, because Allah (Glorified and Exalted is He!), out of His wisdom, has placed within every land particular fruits that are beneficial to the people of that locality when [eaten] in season; and so eating them becomes a means of their good health and well-being, and suffices them from many medicines. Seldom does a person avoid the fruits of his region for fear of sickness except that he becomes one of the sickest of people in his body, and the furthest of them from good health and strength. Fruits will therefore be a beneficial medicine for the one who eats them in the appropriate amount, time, and manner.[460]

460 Shaykh ʿAbdullāh b. Saʿīd al-Laḥjī notes in *Muntahā al-sūl* that there are a number of other fruits that the Prophet ate.
Figs: Ibn al-Sunnī and Abū Nuʿaym narrated on the authority of Abū Dharr who said, "The Prophet was gifted a tray of figs…"
Raisins: Aḥmad narrated in his *Musnad* that the Prophet entered the home of Saʿd b. ʿUbāda and Saʿd presented him some raisins from which he ate.
Truffles: Al-Ṭabarānī narrated that truffles from Ta'if were brought to the Prophet.
Pomegranate: Ibn Ḥibbān narrated that a pomegranate was brought to the Prophet on Day of Arafat and he ate it. [t]

SECTION FIVE

The Description of the Drinks & Drinking Bowl of the Prophet ﷺ

ʿĀʾISHA, THE MOTHER of the Believers ﷺ, said, "The most beloved of drinks to the Messenger of Allah ﷺ was that which was cold and sweet."[461] The Messenger of Allah ﷺ would drink cold water infused with honey.

Jābir related that Prophet ﷺ and another Companion of his went to see a man from the Helpers. The Prophet ﷺ greeted the man and the man replied as he was moving water in his orchard.[462] The Prophet ﷺ then said to him, "If you have some water kept overnight in a water-skin [let us have a drink], otherwise we will drink directly with our mouths [and will not use a vessel or our hands]." The man said, "I have some water that was kept overnight in a water-skin." They went to a shady area of the orchard and the man poured water into a vessel and then milked a house-sheep of his and put the milk in it, then the Prophet ﷺ drank.[463]

461 Al-Tirmidhī, *Shamāʾil*.

462 Commentators say he was either drawing water out from a well or irrigating his crops by moving water through the irrigation canals in his orchard. [t]

463 Al-Bukhārī, *Ṣaḥīḥ*.

When Messenger of Allah ﷺ would finish using a tooth-stick (*siwāk*) he would give it to the eldest person present, and when he would take a drink he would give it to the person on his right side.[464]

The Prophet ﷺ would sip water and not gulp it.[465]

The Prophet ﷺ would give his leftover food to the one who was on his right side. If there was someone on his left who was of a higher rank, he would say to the one on his right, "It is the prophetic wont (*sunna*) that it be given to you, but if you wish I will prefer them [to the left]."[466]

Ibn ʿAbbās ﷺ reported, "Khālid b. al-Walīd and I went along with the Messenger of Allah ﷺ as he went to see Maymūna. She brought us a vessel full of milk. The Messenger of Allah ﷺ drank from it and I was to his right and Khālid was to his left. He said to me, 'The drink is yours, though if you want you can give it to Khālid.' I said, 'I am not about to give up your leftovers for anyone else!' The Messenger of Allah ﷺ said, 'The one whom Allah gives food should say "O Allah, bless us in it and give us to eat from what is better than it." And the one to whom Allah gives drink should say "O Allah, bless us in it and increase us in it."' Then the Messenger of Allah ﷺ said, 'There is nothing that takes the place of food and drink besides milk.'"[467]

The Prophet ﷺ would drink while sitting, and that was his custom. This was narrated by Muslim. In another narration from Muslim it states that the Prophet ﷺ forbade drinking while standing. Ibn ʿAbbās ﷺ reported that the Prophet ﷺ drank Zamzam water

464 Al-Muttaqī al-Hindī, *Kanz al-ʿummāl.*

465 Ibn ʿAdī, *al-Kāmil fī al-ḍuʿafāʾ*.

466 Agreed upon.

467 Al-Tirmidhī, *Shamāʾil.*

while standing.[468] Whenever the Prophet ﷺ wanted to give someone a gift he would pour out Zamzam water for him. The Prophet ﷺ would [also] carry Zamzam water. ʿAbdullāh b. ʿAmr b. al-ʿĀṣ ﷺ said, "I saw the Messenger of Allah ﷺ drinking while standing and while sitting."[469]

Nazzāl b. Sabra said, "A jug of water was brought to ʿAlī while he was in the courtyard.[470] He took a handful of water from it and washed his hands. Then he rinsed his mouth, cleared his nose, and wiped his face, arms, and head. Then he drank the remaining water while standing, and said, 'This is the ablution of the one who has vitiated his ritual purity—this is how I saw the Messenger of Allah ﷺ do it.'"[471]

Kabsha ﷺ said, "The Messenger of Allah ﷺ came to my home. He drank from a hanging leather water-skin while standing up. I [later] stood up and cut off the mouth piece of the water-skin."[472] This means she cut the mouth piece to seek blessings and healing from it. A similar narration is ascribed to Umm Sulaym ﷺ.

The Messenger of Allah ﷺ would not breathe into food or drinks, and would not breathe into a vessel.[473] When the Messenger of Allah ﷺ would drink he would take in three sips. He would say, "This is easier, more quenching, and healthier."[474]

468 Ibid.
469 Ibid.
470 The open courtyard in Kufa where he would sit to adjudicate and deliver sermons. [t]
471 Al-Tirmidhī, *Shamāʾil.*
472 Ibid.
473 Al-Muttaqī al-Hindī, *Kanz al-ʿummāl.*
474 Ibn ʿAdī, *al-Kāmil fī al-ḍuʿafāʾ.*

When the Messenger of Allah ﷺ would drink he would take two breaths[475], and sometimes one breath, until he was finished.

The Messenger of Allah ﷺ would drink in three breaths, and when he would bring the vessel close to his mouth he would invoke Allah's name, and when he moved the vessel away from his mouth he would praise Allah. He would do this three times.

The Messenger of Allah ﷺ would not breathe into a container; rather, he would move it away [from his mouth].[476] On one occasion a container was brought to him containing milk and honey, but he refused to drink it, saying, "There are two drinks in one and two foods in one container." Then he said, "I do not forbid it, but I dislike boasting and being subject to reckoning on the morrow due to the excesses of this world, and I love humility, for whoever is humble for Allah's sake shall be elevated by Him."[477]

Fresh water from Buyūt al-Suqyā would be fetched for the Messenger of Allah ﷺ.[478] Another narration has it, "Fresh water from Buyūt al-Suqyā would be sought for the Messenger of Allah."

Ibn al-Qayyim said, "The Messenger of Allah ﷺ did not drink with his meals lest the drink spoil the food, especially if the water was extremely hot or cold, as this is very harmful."

After the Messenger of Allah ﷺ would drink water he would say, "All praise is to Allah who supplied us a fresh

475 Al-Tirmidhī, *Shamāʾil*.

476 Al-ʿIrāqī, *al-Mughnī ʿan ḥaml al-asfār fī al-asfār*.

477 Al-Mundhirī, *al-Targhīb wa al-tarhīb*.

478 Abū Dāwūd, Sunan. Buyūt al-Suqyā was a well on the outskirts of Medina. [t]

drink out of His mercy, and did not make it salty and bitter due to our sins."[479]

As for the drinking bowl of the Messenger of Allah ﷺ, it has been narrated that Thābit [al-Bunānī] said, "Anas b. Mālik took out for us a thick wooden drinking bowl lined with iron. He said, 'O Thābit, this is the drinking bowl of the Messenger of Allah ﷺ; I had given the Messenger of Allah ﷺ all of his drinks with it: water, *nabīdh*, honey[480], and milk.'"[481] Al-Bājūrī said, "His statement *nabīdh* means a sweet drink made by putting dates in water until the water is sweetened." *Nabīdh* would be prepared for the Messenger of Allah ﷺ during the first part of the night and he would drink from it when he woke up the next morning or during that evening, and the following day up until the afternoon time. If anything was left over he would give it to his servant provided he was not afraid that it had fermented. If it had fermented he would order someone to pour it out.[482] *Nabīdh* is very useful for increasing strength.

Al-Bukhārī narrated from the hadith of ʿĀṣim al-Aḥwal who said, "I saw the Prophet's drinking bowl ﷺ in the possession of Anas b. Mālik. It had cracked so Anas mended it with a silver lining. The bowl was of good quality; it was wide and made of Nuḍār wood. Anas said, 'I had given the Messenger of Allah ﷺ so many drinks from this.' Ibn Sīrīn said, 'There was an iron ring secured around the bowl [to protect it from further cracking],

479 Al-Muttaqī al-Hindī, *Kanz al-ʿummāl.*

480 That is, water infused with honey. [t]

481 Al-Tirmidhī, *Shamāʾil.*

482 Muslim, *Ṣaḥīḥ.*

so Anas wanted to replace it with either a gold or silver ring, but Abū Ṭālḥa protested, "Do not change anything that the Messenger of Allah ﷺ has made!" and so he left it as was."' Nuḍār wood is pure and unblemished wood of any type of tree. It is also said that the drinking bowl was made from the *nabaʿ* tree[483], or from tamarisk. It was a yellowish color.

The Messenger of Allah ﷺ also had a glass bowl from which he would drink.[484]

The Messenger of Allah ﷺ liked to perform ablutions from a brass vessel.[485]

The Messenger of Allah ﷺ also had a bowl from date-palm wood that he kept underneath his bed. He would urinate in it at night.[486]

The Messenger of Allah ﷺ had a washing vessel made of baked clay that he would use for performing ablutions and drinking. People would send out their young pre-pubescent children and they would go the Prophet ﷺ and not be turned away; if they found any leftover water in his washing vessel they would drink it and wipe it on their faces and bodies, seeking blessings therefrom.[487]

After the Messenger of Allah ﷺ finished performing the Morning Prayer, the servants of the people of Medina would come to him with their vessels filled with water. When one of these vessels would be brought to him he

483 A certain type of tree that grows in arid regions and from whose wood arrow shafts are made. [t]

484 Ibn Saʿd, *Ṭabaqāt*. This glass bowl was gifted to the Prophet ﷺ by the Negus of Abyssinia. [t]

485 Ibid.

486 Abū Dāwūd, *Sunan*.

487 Al-Shaʿrānī, *Kashf al-ghumma*.

would submerge his hand in it.[488] The Messenger of Allah ﷺ would send for washing vessels and would drink the water contained in them, hoping that the hands of the Muslims are blessed[489] through that.[490]

488 Aḥmad, *Musnad*.
489 That is, the Prophet ﷺ would drink from the washing vessels in hope that the hands of those who carry them will be blessed. [t]
490 Abū Nuʿaym, *Ḥilyat al-Awliyāʾ*.

SECTION SIX

The Description of the Prophet's Sleep ﷺ

[Al-Qasṭalānī] said in *al-Mawāhib*:

The Prophet ﷺ would sleep in the first part of the night, and would wake up in the first part of the second half of the night, after which he would get up, brush his teeth with a tooth-stick, and perform ablutions. It was not his wont to take more sleep than was needed, though he did not deny himself sleep in the amount needed either. He would sleep on his right side and would retire while invoking Allah Most High until he fell asleep. He would not retire for the night with a belly full of food and drink...

The Prophet ﷺ would sometimes sleep on bedding, sometimes on a leather mat, and sometimes on a palm mat, and sometimes on the ground. The Prophet's bedding was made from tanned skin with palm-tree fiber as its stuffing. He also had a thick and coarse bedding that he would sleep on.

The Prophet ﷺ would sleep in the first part of the night and keep awake in the last part of it.

The Prophet ﷺ would not go to sleep until first brushing his teeth.[491] He would not sleep during the night or the day except that he would brush his teeth upon waking. He would not go to sleep except that a tooth-stick would be near his head, and when he would wake up the first thing he would do is brush his teeth.[492]

He would brush his teeth frequently during the night.[493]

When the Messenger of Allah ﷺ wanted to sleep, he would place his right hand under his [right] cheek and then say three times, "O Allah, save me from Your punishment on the Day You resurrect Your servants!"[494] When the Messenger of Allah ﷺ would retire to his bed he would place his hand under his cheek and then say, "In Your name, O Allah, I live, and in Your name I die." And when he would wake up he would say, "All praise is due to Allah who has brought us to life after causing us to die, and unto Him is the ultimate return."[495]

When the Messenger of Allah ﷺ would retire to his bed he would say, "In the name of Allah I lay on my side. O Allah, forgive me my sin, expel my devil, redeem me, make my scale heavy, and make me among the Loftiest Assembly."[496]

When the Messenger of Allah ﷺ would retire to his bed he would recite "*Say, 'O you who disbelieve…'*" (Chapter al-Kāfirūn) till the end.[497]

491 Al-Bukhārī, *Ṣaḥīḥ*.
492 Aḥmad, *Musnad*.
493 Al-Haythamī, *Majmaʿ al-zawāʾid*.
494 Abū Dāwūd, *Sunan*.
495 Al-Bukhārī, *Ṣaḥīḥ*.
496 Abū Dāwūd, *Sunan*.
497 Al-Haythamī, *Majmaʿ al-zawāʾid*.

ʿĀʾisha said, "Every night when the Messenger of Allah ﷺ would retire to his bed he would join his hands together, lightly blow spittle in them, and recite in them *'Say, "He is Allah, the One..."'* (Chapter al-Ikhlāṣ), *'Say, "I seek refuge with the Lord of the daybreak..."'* (Chapter al-Falaq), and *'Say, "I seek refuge with the Lord of mankind..."'* (Chapter al-Nās); then he would wipe his hands over whatever parts of his body he was able, starting with his head and face and then the front of his body. He would do this three times."[498]

The Prophet ﷺ would not go to sleep until he read the Chapter of Banū Isrāʾil (Sūra al-Isrāʾ) and the Chapter of the Crowds (Sūra al-Zumar).[499]

The Prophet ﷺ would not go to sleep until he read the Chapter *Alif.Lām.Mīm* Prostration (Sūra al-Sajda) and the Chapter of Dominion (Sūra al-Mulk).[500]

Whenever one of the Prophet's wives wished to go to sleep, the Prophet ﷺ would instruct her to praise Allah[501] thirty-three times, glorify Allah[502] thirty-three times, and laud Allah's greatness[503] thirty-three times.[504]

Anas said, "When the Messenger of Allah ﷺ would retire to his bed he would say, 'All praise is due to Allah who has provided us food and drink, who has provided for our needs and returned us to our dwellings,

498 Al-Tirmidhī, *Shamāʾil.*
499 Al-Tirmidhī, *al-Jāmiʿ.*
500 Aḥmad, *Musnad.*
501 To say *al-Ḥamdu Lillāh.* [t]
502 To say *Subḥān Allāh.* [t]
503 To say *Allāhu Akbar.* [t]
504 Al-Muttaqī al-Hindī, *Kanz al-ʿummāl.*

for how many are those with none to suffice them or return them."[505]

ʿĀʾisha ﷺ said, "When the Messenger of Allah ﷺ would turn in the middle of the night he would say, 'There is no god but Allah, the One (al-Wāḥid), the Dominator (al-Qahhār), the Lord of the heavens and the earth and all that is in between them, the Almighty, the Forgiving.'"[506]

When the Messenger of Allah ﷺ would wake up in the middle of the night he would say, "O Lord, forgive and show mercy, and guide to the most upright path."[507]

Abū Qatāda ﷺ related, "When the Prophet ﷺ would take rest at the end of a day's journey he would go to sleep while lying on his right side, and when he would take rest shortly before daybreak he would put his arms up[508] and put his head in his hands."[509]

When the Messenger of Allah ﷺ wanted to go to sleep after having sexual relations he would perform ablutions like those made for prayer, and if he wanted to eat or drink after having sexual relations he would wash his hands and then eat and drink.[510]

When the Messenger of Allah ﷺ wanted to go to sleep after having intimate relations he would wash his private area and perform ablutions.

505 Al-Tirmidhī, *Shamāʾil*.
506 Al-Ḥākim, *al-Mustadrak*.
507 Al-Muttaqī al-Hindī, *Kanz al-ʿummāl*.
508 He ﷺ would lie down with his arms behind his head, since this prevents deep sleep. [t]
509 Al-Tirmidhī, *Shamāʾil*.
510 Muslim, *Ṣaḥīḥ*.

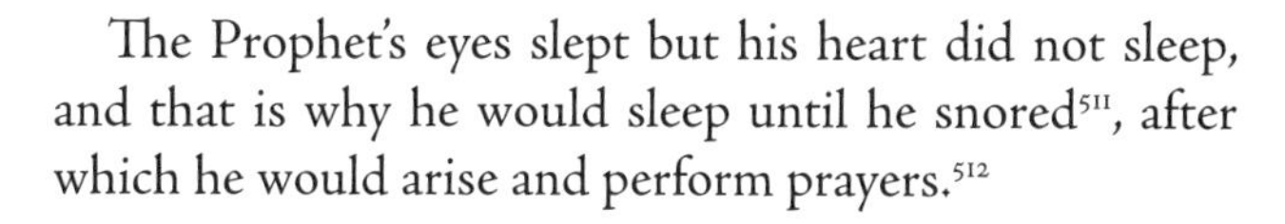

The Prophet's eyes slept but his heart did not sleep, and that is why he would sleep until he snored[511], after which he would arise and perform prayers.[512]

511 Some of scholars have mentioned that the Prophet's snoring was not a respiratory defect, and was rather a form of glorification (*tasbīḥ*). [t]

512 Ibn Abī Shayba, *Muṣannaf*.

Chapter Five

THE DESCRIPTION OF THE CHARACTER OF THE MESSENGER OF ALLAH 

SECTION ONE

The Description of the Prophet's Character ﷺ

Qāḍī ʿIyāḍ said in *al-Shifā*:

> Wahb b. Munabbih said, "I have read seventy-one sacred scriptures and found mentioned in all of them that the Prophet ﷺ is the strongest of people in intellect and the best of them in opinion." Another narration has it, "I found mentioned in all of them [the scriptures] that the intellectual faculties Allah Most High has given to all of mankind, from the beginning of the world till its end, are but like a grain of sand in comparison to the intellect of the Prophet ﷺ."[513]

Al-Qasṭalānī mentioned in his *al-Mawāhib* a narration from [al-Suhrawardī's] *ʿAwārif al-maʿārif*:

> "Sagacity and intelligence are one hundred parts. Ninety-nine parts are within the Prophet ﷺ and one part is within the believers."

513 Abū Nuʿaym, *Ḥilyat al-Awliyāʾ*.

Qāḍī ʿIyāḍ said:

Whoever contemplates the Prophet's excellent management of the Arabs—who were like wild and scattered beasts, and who had repulsive and aloof natures—and how he led them and bore patiently with their boorishness and harms until they began to follow him and rally under him and fight against their own families and fathers and sons for his sake, and how they preferred him over their own selves and emigrated from their homelands and beloveds for his pleasure—all this despite him not having prior experience, and despite him not reading books from where the narratives of the past nations could have been learned. Indeed, if you contemplate these things you will come to the realization that he is the most intelligent of all of creation! Because his intellect ﷺ is the most expansive of intellects, it should come as no surprise that his noble qualities of character were comprehensive and unlimited.

The Prophet's character ﷺ was the Quran. Imam al-Ghazālī said:

Saʿd b. Hishām said, "I went to see ʿĀʾisha—may Allah be pleased with her and her father—and asked about the character of Allah's Messenger ﷺ, whereupon she said, 'Do you not read the Quran?' 'Of course,' I said. Then she said, 'The character of Allah's Messenger was the Quran.'"

The Quran had inculcated him [ﷺ] with propriety through the likes of Allah's words: "*Keep to forgiveness, enjoin kindness and turn away from the ignorant"*[514]; *"Allah commands justice and excellence and giving to relatives; and He forbids indecency, evil and transgression"*[515]; *"Bear with patience whatever befalls you, for that is of the matters that determine affairs"*[516]; *"And for the one who is patient and forgives, that is of the matters that determine affairs"*[517]; *"So pardon them and forgive them, for certainly Allah loves those who act with excellence"*[518]; *"And let them pardon and forgive. Would you not love for Allah to forgive you?"*[519]; *"Repel evil with that which is better, and then the one between you and whom there is enmity will be as an intimate friend"*[520]; *"Those who restrain rage and forgive people—and Allah loves those who those of spiritual excellence"*[521]; and *"Shun much suspicion, for indeed some suspicion is sin. And do not spy on each other, and do not backbite each other."*[522]

[...] The Prophet ﷺ is the primary recipient of this inculcation of propriety and refinement, and then light spreads from him to the whole of creation. As such, he was inculcated with propriety by the Quran, and he in turn inculcated creation with propriety. For this reason he ﷺ said, "I was sent to perfect the noble qualities of character."

514 Quran, 7:199.
515 Ibid., 16:90.
516 Ibid., 31:17.
517 Ibid., 42:43.
518 Ibid., 5:13.
519 Ibid., 24:22.
520 Ibid., 41:34.
521 Ibid., 3:134.
522 Ibid., 49:12.

When Allah perfected his character, He praised him and said, "*And indeed you have an exalted standard of character!*"[523]

It is related from Muʿādh b. Jabal [ﷺ] that the Prophet ﷺ said, 'Verily, Allah has surrounded Islam with noble qualities of character and excellent works."

These qualities include: having good relations with others, performing noble deeds, being affable, bestowing favors, feeding others, extending greetings, visiting a sick Muslim whether he is pious or impious, escorting a Muslim's funeral bier, answering the invitation to partake of food and inviting others to it, pardoning others, making peace between people, possessing munificence and generosity and lenience, initiating the salutations of peace (*salām*), repressing anger, forgiving people, and refraining from what Islam has forbidden, such as vain and frivolous acts, singing, all musical instruments, backbiting, lying, greed, avarice, meanness, artifice, deception, calumny, foul relations, forsaking of family ties, bad character, haughtiness, boasting, conceitedness, arrogance, pride, indecency, foul language, rancor, envy, omen-seeking, transgression, enmity and oppression.

Anas ﷺ said, "He [the Prophet ﷺ] left no beautiful counsel save that he called us to it and commanded us to observe it, and he left nothing that was fraudulent [or he said "shameful" or "despicable"] save that he warned us of it and forbade us from it."

523 Ibid., 68:4.

All of the aforementioned is sufficed by the following verse: "*Allah commands justice and excellence, and giving to near kin, and He forbids vileness and evil and transgression. He exhorts you so that you may take heed.*"[524]

Muʿādh b. Jabal ﷺ said, "The Messenger of Allah ﷺ counselled me, saying: 'O Muʿādh! I counsel you to fear Allah, speak truthfully, fulfil solemn oaths, bear trusts, refrain from perfidiousness, look after the neighbor, extend mercy to the orphan, be affable in speech, extend greetings of peace, perform good works, shorten hopes, remain steadfast in faith, gain deep understanding of the Quran, love the Hereafter, be anxious regarding the Final Reckoning and to be humble; and I forbid you to insult a wise sage, belie a truthful man, obey a sinner, disobey a just leader and to sow corruption; and I counsel you to fear Allah with regard to every stone, tree, or village, and to repent for every sin: a secret repentance for a secret sin and an open repentance for an open sin.'"

This is how the Prophet ﷺ instilled propriety within Allah's servants and invited them to noble qualities of character and good manners!

It is related from al-Ḥasan b. ʿAlī ﷺ, "I asked my uncle Hind b. Abī Hāla[525], who was gifted in describing features (*waṣṣāf*), about the description of the Messenger of Allah ﷺ. I wanted him to describe some of his

524 Ibid., 16:90.

525 He was the brother of Sayyida Fāṭima al-Zahrā ﷺ. She was the son of Sayyida Khadīja b. Khuwaylid ﷺ and Abū Hāla, both of whom were married in the pre-Islamic period of ignorance. [t]

features for me, so he said, 'The Messenger of Allah ﷺ had sublime qualities and was honored as such by others. His face shone like the light of the full moon...'[526]

"I concealed this from al-Ḥusayn for a time, and later, when I narrated it to him, I found that he had beaten me to it; he asked his father [ʿAlī ؓ] about the Prophet's character inside and outside his home, and asked him about his features, and did not omit a single detail. Al-Ḥusayn said, 'I asked my father about how the Messenger of Allah ﷺ was when he would enter his home. He said, "When he entered his home ﷺ he would divide his time into three portions: a portion for [devotions to] Allah, a portion for his family, and a portion for himself. Then he would take the portion that was for himself and divide between himself and the people, giving to the elect what was to be conveyed to the common folk.[527] He would not keep anything from them.[528] His conduct in the portion for his nation was that he would give preference for the people of merit, with his permission, and would apportion his time among them according to their virtue in the religion. Some of them were in need of one thing, others in need of two things, and others with many needs. He would occupy himself with their needs and keep them busy in things that would bring benefit to

526 Here Shaykh Yūsuf al-Nabahānī omits the detailed physical descriptions of the Prophet ﷺ, all of which he mentioned earlier. [t]

527 That is, the Prophet ﷺ would teach the elect among the senior Companions and they would convey his teachings to the common folk who did not have the chance to sit privately with him. [t]

528 That is, the Prophet ﷺ did not keep anything from them of religious counsel and guidance. [t]

them and to the *Umma,* and he would respond to their needs and inform them of what they should do. He would say, 'Let those present among you convey to those who are absent; apprise me of the need of the one who is unable to apprise me himself, for whoever apprises the ruler of the need of one who is unable to convey it, Allah will make his feet firm on the Day of Resurrection.' This was all that was mentioned in his presence, and he would accept nothing but this from anyone. They would enter as seekers and only disperse after having tasted something[529], leaving as guides (i.e., to goodness)."

'Then I asked him how the Messenger of Allah ﷺ was when he left his home and what he would do. He said, "The Messenger of Allah ﷺ would hold his tongue from speaking about anything except that which concerned him. He would bring the people together and would not cause them to scatter. He would honor the nobles of every folk and appoint them over their people. He was cautious of people and on guard with them[530], though without frowning or being discourteous. He would inquire about his Companions when they were not around and ask the elect about the general welfare of others. He would praise what is beautiful and strengthen it, and would condemn what is ugly and weaken it.[531] His

529 Either tasting physically, by partaking of a meal with the Prophet ﷺ, or tasting spiritually, by receiving guidance and openings from him. [t]

530 That is, the Prophet ﷺ was keenly aware of human nature and was never oblivious to the actions, good or bad, of people around him. He would not mix excessively with others lest people become too comfortable in his presence and neglect the high etiquette that is required around him. [t]

531 That is, the Prophet ﷺ would praise what is beautiful and

was the balanced course, unswerving from one extreme to another. He was never remiss[532], fearing that others might become remiss or weary. He was duly prepared for every eventuality. He neither neglected a right nor did he exceed it.[533] Those who were close to him were the choicest of the people, and the most virtuous of them in his sight were those whose sincere counsel was most general[534], and the most esteemed of them in station were those who were most beneficent and helpful to others."

'Then I asked him about the gatherings of the Messenger of Allah ﷺ. He said, "The Messenger of Allah would not rise or sit without invoking Allah. When he would go to sit with a people he would take his seat wherever space remained in the gathering and he would tell others to do the same. He would give everyone sitting with him an ample share of his attention, and the one sitting with him would think that there is no one more honorable in the Prophet's sight than him. Whenever a person would come to him for help he would patiently assist him until it was he [the Prophet ﷺ] who was dismissed. Whenever a person would petition him for a need he would not leave him empty-handed—he would either give him his need or give him a goodly word. In his cheerful smiling countenance and character he became

---

strengthen it with rational and textual proofs, and would condemn what is ugly and weaken it by prohibiting it and discouraging it. [t]

532 That is, in reminding them and guiding them. [t]

533 That is, the Prophet ﷺ neither neglected the rights of others nor did he take from them more than what was required. [t]

534 That is, their advice and counsel was given to the general body of the Muslims, since the Prophet ﷺ said, "The religion in its entirety is sincere counsel." [t]

like a father unto them, and they all became equal in his eyes when it came to the fulfilment of rights. His gatherings were gatherings of forbearance and shyness, patience and trust. Voices were not raised, sanctities were not violated[535], and odious behavior was not displayed. They were equal and only superior to one another on the basis of God-consciousness. They were humble; they would show respect to the elders, have mercy upon the young, give preference to those in need, and look after the strangers.[536]'""

The Messenger of Allah ﷺ never let a moment pass by without righteous deeds for the sake of Allah Most High, or what was necessary for his personal needs.

The Prophet ﷺ was the best of mankind in character.

The Messenger of Allah ﷺ was always smiling, affable in his disposition.

[Al-Bājūrī said:] "They [scholars] have defined good character with the following: interacting with others in a way that is beautiful; smiling and being gentle towards others; bearing the annoyances of others and being kind toward them; forbearance; patience; avoiding high-handedness and arrogance toward others; eschewing boorishness, anger, and revenge."

ʿAlī ﷺ said, "The breast of the Messenger of Allah ﷺ was the most generous of breasts, and he was the most truthful of men in speech. He was the gentlest of people in nature and the kindest of them in companionship.

535 That is, people would not backbite or speak about the wives and families of others. [t]

536 The final phrase "look after strangers" can be read in two ways: 1) to look after strangers visiting from distant lands, 2) to look after, by memorising and preserving, the obscure details of prophecy given to them by the Messenger of Allah ﷺ. [t]

Whoever saw him unexpectedly would be awe-stricken, and whoever got to know him would love him. Whoever described him would say, 'I saw neither before him nor after him anyone like him.'"[537]

Anas said, "The Messenger of Allah was the most knowledgeable, conscientious, noble, just, forbearing, and chaste of people. His hand never touched the hand of a woman over whom he did not have possession or to whom he was not married, or who was not an unmarriageable kin (*maḥram*).[538] Anas also said, "The Messenger of Allah was the best and most generous and brave of people."[539]

The Messenger of Allah was the most merciful, providential, and beneficial of men to people. He was the best of men toward people and the most patient of men with the ills of people. Khārija b. Zayd b. Thābit said, "A group of people went to see Zayd b. Thābit . The said to him, 'Narrate to us some traditions about the Messenger of Allah .' He said, 'What shall I narrate to you? I was his neighbor. When revelation would descend upon him he would send for me to write it down. When we would speak about worldly matters he would speak about them as well, and when we would speak about the Hereafter he would participate with us. When we would speak about food he would speak about it likewise—so shall I narrate all of this to you of the Messenger of Allah?'"[540]

The Companions of the Messenger of Allah would occasionally rehearse poetry in his presence and humorously recall events that took place in the pre-

537 Aḥmad, *Musnad*.

538 Al-Shaʿrānī, *Kashf al-ghumma*.

539 Aḥmad, *Musnad*.

540 Al-Tirmidhī, *Shamāʾil*.

Islamic period of ignorance (*jāhilīya*). The Prophet ﷺ would smile as they would laugh and did not rebuke them except for what was unlawful (*ḥarām*).[541]

Of all people, the Messenger of Allah ﷺ was the most constant in smiling and laughter in the presence of his Companions, ever expressing amazement with what they spoke of to him, always mingling with them. He would sometimes smile till his molars showed. Out of their respect for and emulation of him, his Companions' laugh was but a smile.[542]

They [his Companions] mentioned, "One day a Bedouin came to the Prophet ﷺ but his demeanor had changed and was unrecognizable to his Companions. The man wanted to ask something of the Prophet ﷺ but they said, 'O Bedouin! Don't do it, for we do not recognize his demeanor.' To this the Bedouin replied, 'By Him Who sent him with the truth as a Prophet, I will not leave him until he smiles!' He then said, 'O Messenger of God! It has reached us that the Anointed [the Anti-Christ (*Dajjāl*)] shall bring *tharīd* to people who are dying of hunger. May my father and mother be sacrificed for you! Do you think I should abstain from his *tharīd* out of restraint (*taʿaffuf*) and dignity until I die of emaciation, or should I eat of his *tharīd* and when I am satiated I will believe in Allah and reject him?' Upon hearing this, the Prophet ﷺ smiled until his molar teeth showed and said, 'No. Instead, Allah shall suffice you with that by which He suffices the believers.'"

The Messenger of Allah ﷺ would act tenderly toward his Companions, soothing their concerns and inquiring about those who were absent from his gathering. He

541 Al-Bayhaqī, *al-Sunan al-kubrā*.

542 Al-Zabīdī, *Itḥāf al-sādāt al-muttaqīn*.

would often say to individuals among them, "Perhaps, dear brother, you have encountered something from me or from our brethren."[543]

When the Messenger of Allah ﷺ did not see one of his brethren for three days he would inquire about him. If the person was absent [traveling] he would supplicate for him; if he was around he would go see him; and if he was sick he go and visit him.[544]

The Messenger of Allah ﷺ would go to his Companions with a smiling and cheerful countenance, till each of them thought that he was the most honored of his Companions in his sight.[545]

The Messenger of Allah ﷺ would give every person who sat with him an ample share of cheerful demeanor till the person would think that he is the most honored of people in his sight.[546]

ᶜAmr b. al-ᶜĀṣ said, "The Messenger of Allah ﷺ would turn his face to and speak with the worst of a people in order to bring their hearts together.[547] He would also turn his face towards me and speak with me in such a manner that I began to think that I was best of the people. I asked him, 'O Messenger of Allah, am I better or Abū Bakr?' 'Abū Bakr,' he replied. I asked, 'O Messenger of Allah, am I better or ᶜUmar?' 'ᶜUmar,' he replied. I asked, 'O Messenger of Allah, am I better or ᶜUthmān?' 'ᶜUthmān,' he replied. After I asked [these questions to] the Messenger of Allah and he told me

543 That is, something that has disquieted or angered you. [t]

544 Abū Yaᶜlā, *Musnad*.

545 Al-Shaᶜrānī, *Kashf al-ghumma*.

546 Ibid.

547 That is, to strengthen their Islam or prevent them from evil. [t]

the truth I wished I had not asked him."[548]

The Messenger of Allah ﷺ would give each person who sat with him an ample share of his face[549], such that it was as if his sitting, listening, and conversing, and his subtle beauties and guidance were exclusively for that person. In addition to that, his gatherings were gatherings of shyness, humility, and trust. Allah Most High said, "*It was by a mercy from Allah that you were lenient with them. Had you been stern and harsh of heart they would have certainly dispersed from your midst.*" (Quran 3:159)

The Messenger of Allah ﷺ never talked to anyone in a way the person disliked. Anas ﷺ related, "A man once entered in the presence of the Messenger of Allah ﷺ while wearing a garment with traces of yellow dye. The Messenger of Allah ﷺ seldom talked to anyone in a way the person disliked, so when the man finally left he said to some of the people, 'Would that you tell this man to forgo this garment of yellow dye.'"[550]

Al-Bājūrī said:

> What this means is that he [ﷺ] would seldom confront a person with something he disliked. This does not contradict what was reported from ʿAbdullāh b. ʿAmr b. al-ʿĀṣ, who said, "The Messenger of Allah ﷺ saw me wearing two garments dyed in saffron, and he said, 'These two are from the garments of the disbelievers, so do not wear them.'" Another narration has it, "I asked, 'Should I wash them?' He replied, 'Nay, you should burn them.'" (Perhaps the command to burn them is interpreted

548 Al-Tirmidhī, *Shamāʾil*.
549 That is, his attention. [t]
550 Al-Tirmidhī, *Shamāʾil*.

as a rebuke of sorts.) This substantiates the position those scholars who forbade the wearing of saffron garments (though the majority of scholars hold that it is offensive (*makrūh*)).

The Messenger of Allah ﷺ would not confront anyone with something the person disliked, nor would he address a specific person when delivering an exhortation. Instead, he would speak in general terms.

When a person would [do or say] something [unbecoming] and it reached the attention of the Messenger of Allah ﷺ, he would not say "What is the matter with so-and-so?" rather he would say, "What is the matter with a people who say such-and-such?"[551]

The Prophet's manner of rebuke was through intimation. He would say, "What is the matter with a folk who stipulate conditions not found in the Book of Allah? ..."[552]

When the Messenger of Allah ﷺ would see someone do something inappropriate he would not allow anyone rush to censure him until he first ascertained the matter himself and taught the person with propriety and gentleness.[553]

The Messenger of Allah ﷺ would never punish someone based [solely] on an accusation, nor would he accept the charges of one person against another.[554]

The Messenger of Allah ﷺ would say, "Let none of you inform me of anything [negative] concerning one of

551 Abū Dāwūd, *Sunan*.

552 Agreed upon.

553 Al-Shaʿrānī, *Kashf al-ghumma*.

554 That is, without ascertaining the truth and investigating the charges. [t]

my Companions, for I like to come out to you with a sound breast (*salāmat al-ṣadr*)."[555]

When the Messenger of Allah ﷺ would send out one of his Companions to do something on his behalf[556] he would say, "Give glad tidings and do not drive people away; make things easy and do not make things difficult."[557]

When the Messenger of Allah ﷺ would meet with his Companions he would not shake their hands until he greeted them with peace.[558] Whenever he met with one of his Companions, the Messenger of Allah ﷺ would be the first to initiate the shaking of hands; he would then take his Companion's hand and clasp it, fingers intertwined, strengthening his grasp over it.

When any of the Prophet's Companions would encounter him, he [the Companion] would stand up and the Prophet would stand up with him, and he would not leave the Companion until the Companion left him [on his own].[559]

When one of his Companions would meet him and extend his hand, the Messenger of Allah ﷺ would extend his hand and would shake it and would not release it until the Companion released his first. And when he would meet with one of his Companions and lend him his ear—that is, for the Companion to whisper something secretly to him—he would not remove his ear until the Companion moved away from him, meaning

555 Al-Tirmidhī, *Sunan*.

556 That is, when he would send one of them out to invite people to Islam or take command over an army, etc. [t]

557 Al-Bukhārī, *Ṣaḥīḥ*.

558 Al-Ṭabarānī, *al-Muʿjam al-kabīr*.

559 Ibn Saʿd, *Ṭabaqāt*.

he would not move his ear away from the Companion's mouth until the Companion finished telling his secret.

When the Messenger of Allah ﷺ would meet a man from his Companions he would shake his hand and supplicate for him.[560]

No one of his Companions—or anyone else—invited him but that he said, "At your service (*labbayk*)!"[561]

The Messenger of Allah ﷺ used to address his Companions by their agnomens (*kunyas*) so as to honor them and win their hearts' affection. He would confer an agnomen on the one who did not have an agnomen and would address him by it. He would also confer agnomens on women, both those with children and those without, starting with the latter. He would also confer agnomens on young children, softening their hearts by it.[562]

When the Messenger of Allah ﷺ would pass by young children he would greet them and pat their heads.

When the Messenger of Allah ﷺ would return from a journey he would be received and welcomed by the young children.[563]

The Messenger of Allah ﷺ was the most merciful of people toward young children and dependents.[564]

Infants would be brought to the Messenger of Allah ﷺ and he would bless them, perform the *taḥnīk*[565], and pray for them.

560 Al-Nasāʾī, *Sunan*.

561 Al-Shaʿrānī, *Kashf al-ghumma*.

562 Ibid.

563 Aḥmad, *Musnad*.

564 Ibn ʿAsākir, *Tārīkh Dimashq*.

565 That is, take a date or something sweet and chew it and place it on the infant's palate. This is one of the Sunnas of welcoming a newborn. [t]

The Messenger of Allah ﷺ would visit the Helpers (Anṣār) and greet their young children and rub their heads.

Yūsuf b. ʿAbdullāh b. Salām رضي الله عنه said, "The Messenger of Allah ﷺ named me Yūsuf, seated me in his lap, and rubbed my head."[566]

The Messenger of Allah ﷺ would play with Zaynab the daughter of Umm Salama and say repeatedly, "Little Zaynab, little Zaynab (*Zuwaynab*)!"[567]

The Messenger of Allah ﷺ would carry al-Ḥasan and al-Ḥusayn on his back while crawling around on his hands and feet. He would say to them, "What an excellent camel you have! What excellent riders you are!" He would perhaps have them take turns.[568] On one occasion, as the Messenger of Allah ﷺ was prostrating [in prayer], al-Ḥasan entered and climbed onto his back. The Messenger of Allah ﷺ lengthened his prostration until al-Ḥasan climbed down. When he finished [the prayer] some of his Companions said, "O Messenger of Allah! You lengthened your prostration." He said, "My son made me his mount and I disliked to rush him."[569] That is, he mounted the Prophet's back [ﷺ] as if he was a mount.

Ibn Masʿūd رضي الله عنه said, "The Messenger of Allah ﷺ was once praying while al-Ḥasan and al-Ḥusayn were playing and sitting on his back."[570]

Abū Hurayra رضي الله عنه said, "I saw the Messenger of Allah

566 Al-Tirmidhī, *Shamāʾil*.

567 Al-Ḍiyāʾ al-Maqdisī, al-Mukhtāra. *Zuwaynab* is the diminutive form (*taṣghīr*) of the name Zaynab. [t]

568 Al-Ṭabarānī, *al-Muʿjam al-kabīr*.

569 Al-Qasṭalānī, *al-Mawāhib al-laduniyya*.

570 Al-Muttaqī al-Hindī, *Kanz al-ʿummāl*.

ﷺ take al-Ḥasan b. ᶜAlī and place his [al-Ḥasan's] legs on his knees and say, 'Climb up, climb up O little-eyed one, O *ḥuzuqqa*!'" [Ibn Manẓūr] said in *Lisān al-ᶜArab*:

> This hadith shows that the Prophet ﷺ would swing al-Ḥasan and al-Ḥusayn around and say "*Ḥuzuqqa*! Climb up, O little-eyed one!" *Ḥuzuqqa* means a weak person whose footsteps are close together. [Al-Ḥasan] would climb up till his feet reached the Prophet's chest ﷺ. Ibn al-Athīr said, "The Prophet ﷺ mentioned this out of playfulness and tenderness towards him [al-Ḥasan]."

The Messenger of Allah ﷺ would honor the people of virtue for their good character, and would win the people of nobility over through kind acts. He treated his kindred well, without preferring them to one who is more virtuous than they.[571]

The Messenger of Allah ﷺ would honor Banū Hāshim[572] and was the most intensely benevolent of all people toward al-ᶜAbbās[573], whom he honored like a son honors his father.[574]

The Messenger of Allah ﷺ would initiate the greetings of peace with whomever he met, and when he would grasp someone's hand he would walk with him till it was the person who left.

When the Messenger of Allah ﷺ would bid a man farewell he would grasp his hand and not let go of it until the man let go of his hand, and he would supplicate, "I

571 Al-Shaᶜrānī, *Kashf al-ghumma*.
572 Al-Munāwī, *Kunūz al-ḥaqāʾiq*.
573 Ibid.
574 Al-Ḥākim, *al-Mustadrak*.

entrust to Allah your faith, what you have left behind, and your final actions."[575]

No one ever sat in the Prophet's presence while he was praying but that he would shorten his prayer and turn to the person and say, "Have you any need?" And after fulfilling his need the Prophet ﷺ would recommence his prayers.[576]

The Messenger of Allah ﷺ would honor those who visited him, often spreading out his garment and having sit upon it those with whom he had no ties of kinship or suckling.[577] He would prefer his guest [over himself] by [offering him] the cushion on which he reclined; if the guest refused he would urge him until he accepted it.[578]

Anas b. Mālik رضي الله عنه said, "I served the Messenger of Allah ﷺ for ten years and never once did he say 'Fie!' to me, nor did he ever say to me if I did something 'Why did you do that?' or to something I did not do 'Why did you not do that?'"[579] Anas also said, "I served the Messenger of Allah ﷺ when I was eight years old, and continued to serve him for ten years, and not once did he ever blame me for anything. And if any of his family blamed me for something he would say to them 'Leave him be, for if something is preordained it will come to pass.'"

In [*Mishkāt*] *al-maṣābīḥ* there is another report from Anas, who said, "The Messenger of Allah ﷺ was the best of people in character. One day he sent me on an errand but I said, 'By Allah, I will not go'—even though inwardly I intended to go where the Messenger of Allah

575 Al-Tirmidhī, *al-Daʿawāt*.

576 Al-Shaʿrānī, *Kashf al-ghumma*.

577 Ibid.

578 Ibid.

579 Al-Tirmidhī, *Shamāʾil*.

ﷺ ordered me to go. I went out on the errand and [on my way] I passed by some young children playing in the market. Suddenly, the Messenger of Allah ﷺ was standing behind me and took me by the neck. I looked up at him and saw that he was smiling. He say, 'O Unays[580], did you go where I told you to go?' I replied, 'Yes, O Messenger of Allah, I am going.'"[581]

Anas ﷺ also reported, "I was once walking with the Prophet ﷺ and he was wearing a Najrani mantle with a thick hem. A Bedouin followed him and tugged on his mantle so roughly that I noticed that the side of the Prophet's shoulder had a mark from the mantle. The Bedouin demanded, 'O Muḥammad, give me some of Allah's wealth that is with you!' The Messenger of Allah turned to him and smiled and then ordered that he be given something."

The Messenger of Allah ﷺ was neither coarse nor harsh. ʿĀʾisha, the Mother of the Believers ﷺ, said, "The Messenger of Allah ﷺ was not harsh, coarse, or boisterous in market places. He did not requite evil with evil, but rather he pardoned and forgave."

[Al-Ghazālī] said in *Iḥyāʾ ʿulūm al-dīn*:

> In the Torah, Allah (Exalted is He!) described the Prophet ﷺ before he was sent, saying, "Muḥammad is the Messenger of Allah; he is My chosen servant. He is not harsh, coarse, or boisterous in market places. He does not requite evil with evil, but rather he pardons and forgives. His place of birth is Mecca, his place of emigration is Ṭāba [Medina] and his kingdom is in the Levant (Shām). He

580 A diminutive form of the name Anas. [t]

581 Al-Baghawī, *Sharḥ al-Sunna*.

clothes himself with the loincloth, and he and those in his company are callers to the Quran and knowledge. He washes his extremities." This is also his description in the Gospel.

The Messenger of Allah ﷺ never behaved coarsely with anyone, even if a person acted in a way that would merit coarseness, and he would accept the excuse of the one who begged his pardon even if the person did what he did.

When the Messenger of Allah ﷺ endured annoyance he would say, "May Allah show mercy to the brother of Mūsā; he suffered much greater than this and he maintained patience."[582]

The Messenger of Allah ﷺ would watch permissible games and did not disapprove of them, and when voices would be raised in his presence uttering boorish words he would tolerate it and not take [them] to task.

Whenever the Messenger of Allah ﷺ was asked to invoke against someone, he would turn it from an invocation *against* to an invocation *for* the person.

The Messenger of Allah ﷺ never once struck a woman or a servant or anyone else unless he was in Jihad. Anas ﷺ said, "When a servant would do something to anger the Prophet ﷺ, he would say, 'Were is not for fear of retribution on the Day of Resurrection I would have hit you with this tooth-stick!'"[583]

When the Prophet's molar tooth was broken during the Battle of Uḥud it weighed heavily on his Companions, and so they said, "Would that you invoke a curse against them!" He responded, "I was only sent as an inviter and

582 Al-Shaʿrānī, *Kashf al-ghumma*.
583 Ibid.

a mercy; I was not sent as a curser. O Allah, guide my people for they do not know!"[584]

ʿĀʾisha ﷺ said, "I never saw the Messenger of Allah ﷺ exact revenge for a personal injustice done against him, so long as the sanctities of Allah were not violated. If any of Allah's sanctities were violated he would be the angriest of people. He was never put in the position to choose between two things except that chose the easiest, unless that choice entailed sin, in which case he would be the furthest removed from it.[585]

The Messenger of Allah ﷺ never got angry for himself or exacted revenge for himself; he would only become angry if the sanctities of Allah were violated, and nothing would settle his anger until he established what was right. When he would become angry he would turn his face away.[586]

ʿĀʾisha ﷺ related, "A man once sought permission from the Messenger of Allah ﷺ to see him while I was with him. He said, 'How wretched a man among his folk!' or he said 'How wretched a brother among his folk!' Then he granted the man permission to enter and spoke softly to him. When the man left I said, 'O Messenger of Allah, you said what you said [earlier] and then you spoke softly to him [why is that?].' He said, 'O ʿĀʾisha, among the worst of people is he whom others leave (or forsake)[587] in order to avoid his obscenity.'"[588]

584 Al-Qasṭalānī, *al-Mawāhib al-laduniyya*.

585 Al-Tirmidhī, *Shamāʾil*.

586 Because of the Prophet's clemency, when someone upset him he would turn his face away from the person and not give him a displeasing gaze. [t]

587 The narrator was in doubt as to which phrase was used. [t]

588 Al-Tirmidhī, *Shamāʾil*.

[Al-Qasṭalānī] said in *al-Mawāhib*:

This man was ʿUyayna b. Ḥiṣn al-Fazārī. He used to be called "The obeyed fool." Certain incidents took place during the Prophet's life ﷺ and after his passing that indicated that this man's faith was weak, and thus the Prophet's description of him is one of the signs of prophethood.

As for the soft words that were spoken to him after he entered, they were for the sake winning over his heart and sociability (*mudārāt*), which is permissible and perhaps a good practice at times, unlike sycophancy (*mudāhana*). The difference between the two is that sociability is the sacrifice a worldly interest in order to attain either a worldly or a religious benefit, or both together, whereas sycophancy is to sacrifice one's religion for the sake of attaining a worldly benefit. As such, the Prophet ﷺ [only] sacrificed his worldly interest to him by treating him well and speaking softly to him, and despite that he did not compliment the man, so there is no contradiction between what the Prophet said and what he did. What he said concerning the man was true, and how he treated the man was kind company. This man ʿUyayna later left Islam during the reign of [Abū Bakr] al-Ṣiddīq and waged war [against the Muslims], and sometime later returned and embraced Islam once again and participated in some of the conquests during the reign of ʿUmar ؓ.

Ibn al-Athīr said in his book *Usd al-ghāba*, at the end of his biographical entry on Makhrama b. Nawfal ؓ:

> Al-Naḍr b. Shumayl related, "Abū ʿĀmir al-Khazzāz narrated to us on the authority of Abū Yazīd al-Madanī, who related on the authority of ʿĀʾisha, who said, 'Makhrama b. Nawfal came [to see the Prophet ﷺ], and when the Prophet ﷺ heard his voice he said, "How wretched a brother among his folk!" When he came, however, the Prophet brought him near. I said, "O Messenger of Allah, you said what you said to him and then spoke softly to him." He said, "O ʿĀʾisha, among the worst of people is he whom others leave in order to avoid his obscenity."'"
>
> This man Makhrama was of those whose hearts were reconciled. He had a habit of foul speech, so the Prophet ﷺ was safeguarding himself from his tongue.

It seems that the correct view is the one mentioned here by Ibn al-Athīr, namely that the person mentioned in the incident was Makhrama b. Nawfal. On the other hand, it can be said that a similar incident occurred [with ʿUyayna].

Al-Ḥasan b. ʿAlī ؓ related, "Al-Ḥusayn said, 'I asked my father about the conduct (*sīra*) of the Prophet ﷺ in his gatherings. He said, "The Prophet ﷺ was always smiling. He had a soft character and affable disposition. He was neither harsh nor coarse nor boisterous nor obscene, nor was he a fault-finder nor one given to trivial argumentation. He would overlook things he disliked and would not cause others to despair of them; he would simply avoid partaking of them.[589] He forsook

589 For this somewhat recondite phrase the commentators have suggested a number of interpretations. The simplest one, reflect-

three things for himself: disputation, the superfluous, and matters that did not concern him. He [also] forsook three things with respect to people: he would not find fault with anyone, he would not condemn anyone, and he would not pry into the private affairs of others. When he would speak he would only speak about things for which he hoped in a reward from Allah, and when he would speak, those sitting in his company would lower their heads and be so still it was as if birds were perched atop their heads. Only after he would stop talking would they speak. They would not dispute with one another when they would converse in his presence. They would listen attentively to whosoever spoke in his presence until the person was finished. The first of them to speak to the Prophet ﷺ would be the first of them to enter. He ﷺ would smile at what they would laugh at, and he would express amazement with that with which they expressed amazement. He ﷺ would be patient with the boorish speech and requests of strangers, and so it was that his Companions would usher them to the Prophet[590] and he

ed in the translation, is that if the Prophet ﷺ disliked something that was legally neutral he would overlook it, while at the same time he would not cause others to despair of partaking of it. He would simply remain silent and dignified. An alternative wording of this narration says "He would not disappoint"—that is, if something, such as a dish, was presented to him and he disliked it, he would overlook it while at the same time he would not disappoint anyone who wanted to partake of it, by expressing his distaste or disallowing the person from eating it. Another version of al-Tirmidhī's *Shamāʾil* has it, "He would overlook what he liked" without the word "dis". This means he did not go to great lengths to acquire foods that he enjoyed eating. Allah knows best. [t]

590 That is, because strangers would have a tendency to ask very

would say, "If you see a person seeking the fulfilment of a need then help him."[591] He would only accept praise from one who was responding to a favor given.[592] He would not interrupt a person while he was speaking unless the person went too far, in which case he would interrupt it by either prohibiting the person [from speaking in that manner] or getting up to leave.

As for the forbearance of the Messenger of Allah ﷺ, he was the most forbearing of men and the most desirous of pardoning, despite his ability not to [if had so wished]. [So great was his forbearance] that once, when he received some necklaces of gold and silver and began to distribute them to his Companions, there arose a man from the remote desert wastelands who called out, "O Muḥammad! By Allah, if He has commanded you to act justly, then I do not see you acting justly!" Thereupon the Prophet ﷺ said, "Woe unto you! Who will act justly towards you after me?" After the man went away the Prophet ﷺ said, "Bring him back to me gently."[593]

---

direct and even personal questions—questions that the Companions would be too shy to ask—they would happily escort strangers to the Prophet ﷺ so they could benefit from hearing the answers. [t]

591 That is, help the person in need by bringing him to me. [t]

592 This means that the Prophet ﷺ would only accept the praise of a person who was thanking him for a gift or some favor he did for him, this being the Quranic character: "*Do not consider those who love to be praised for what they have not done* [to be free of the punishment in the Hereafter]..." (Quran 3:188) [t]

593 Al-Ḥākim, *al-Mustadrak*.

Jābir reported that on the day of [the Battle of] Ḥunayn, the Prophet ﷺ was distributing silver [held] in Bilāl's garment, whereupon a man said to him, "O Messenger of Allah! Be just!" The Messenger of Allah ﷺ replied, "Woe unto you! Who will act justly if I do not act justly? Had I not acted justly I would have assuredly failed and lost!" At that moment, ʿUmar [b. al-Khaṭṭāb ﵁] stood up and asked, "Shall I not smite his neck, as he is a hypocrite?" The Prophet ﷺ said, "Allah's refuge is sought, that the people should say I kill my companions!"[594]

On one occasion, the Messenger of Allah ﷺ was distributing war booty when a man from the Helpers[595] said, "This distribution is not done sincerely for Allah's sake!" When this was mentioned to the Prophet ﷺ, his face became red and he said, "May Allah show mercy to my brother Mūsā; he suffered much greater than this and he maintained patience."

A Bedouin once urinated inside the Mosque in the presence of the Prophet ﷺ. The Companions thought to stop him, but the Prophet ﷺ said, "Do not stop him." (That is to say, "Do not interrupt his urination".) Then he said to the man, "These mosques are not suited as places of filth, urine, or excrement." And in another narration[596] of this report the Prophet ﷺ said, "Draw people close and do not drive them away."

One day a Bedouin came to the Prophet ﷺ and asked him for something. The Prophet ﷺ gave it to him and

594 Muslim, *Ṣaḥīḥ*.

595 Ibn Saʿd's narration of this incident says that he was Muʿtab b. Qushayr, one of the hypocrites of Medina, not a Helper properly speaking. [t]

596 Al-Bukhārī, *Ṣaḥīḥ*.

asked, "Have I treated you with excellence?" The Bedouin answered, "No. Nor have you acted beautifully!" Upon hearing this, the Muslims became angry and rose against the man, but the Prophet ﷺ signaled for them to desist. Afterwards, the Prophet ﷺ stood up and entered his home and sent more [provisions] to the Bedouin, adding more than [what he gave] the previous time. He later asked the man, "Have I treated you with excellence?" to which the man said, "Yes! May Allah reward you with good on behalf of family and kin!" The Prophet ﷺ said to him, "You uttered a statement earlier and something of it remains fresh in the minds of my Companions; if you like, repeat to them what you said to me [now] so that their feelings against you can leave their breasts." The Bedouin said, "Yes [I'll do so]." The next day, or later that evening, the Bedouin came and the Prophet ﷺ said, "Verily, this Bedouin said what he said, and so we increased the amount of what was given to him, and he said that he was pleased. Is that so?" The Bedouin said, "Yes. May Allah reward you with good on behalf of family and kin!" The Prophet ﷺ said, "The likeness of me and this Bedouin is that of a man who had a she-camel that ran away from him. The people pursued her, which only increased her in avoidance. Thereupon the she-camel's owner cried, 'Leave me to my she-camel, for I am gentle with her and know best [how to retrieve her].' The she-camel's owner then turned to it, took some sweepings for her and gently returned her until she came and kneeled and he saddled her and sat upon her. Had I left you after the man said what he said you would have killed him and he would have entered the Fire!"[597]

597 Al-Bazzār, *Musnad*.

Abū Hurayra ﷺ reported, "I was once with the Prophet ﷺ and he was wearing a mantle with a thick hem. A Bedouin came and tugged on his mantle so roughly that the collar left a mark on the back of the Prophet's neck. The Bedouin demanded, 'O Muḥammad, load up these two camels of mine with some of Allah's wealth that is with you, for you shall not be giving me from your wealth or the wealth of your father!' The Prophet ﷺ was silent for a moment and then he said, 'The wealth is indeed Allah's wealth, and I am His servant.' Then the Prophet ﷺ said, 'Shall you be requited for what you did to me, O Bedouin?' 'No,' replied the Bedouin. 'Why?' asked the Prophet ﷺ. 'Because,' he said, 'you do not respond to a wrong with a wrong!' Upon hearing this, the Prophet smiled and ordered that one of his camels be loaded with barley and the other be loaded with dates."[598]

Al-Ṭabarānī, Ibn Ḥibbān, al-Ḥākim, and al-Bayhaqī all recorded a narration from Zayd b. Saʿna who, as al-Nawawī (may Allah have mercy upon him) said, was the noblest of the learned Jews who embraced Islam. Zayd said, "Apart from two, there were no signs of prophethood except that I could recognize them in the face of Muḥammad ﷺ when I looked at him. There remained but two signs which I had yet to test out[599]: that his forbearance overcomes his anger, and that extreme ignorance only increases him in forbearance. I behaved pleasantly with him in hope of interacting with him and coming to know his forbearance and anger, and so I bought some dates from him that would be delivered to me at a later date. I paid the price for them. Two or three

598 Abū Dāwūd, *Sunan*.

599 Because these signs can only be witnessed when they are experienced. [t]

days before the delivery date I went to the Prophet and pulled him from his shirt and cloak and gave him a stern look and said, 'O Muḥammad! Will you not give me my right? By Allah, you Children of ʿAbd al-Muṭṭalib are a bunch of procrastinators!' ʿUmar said, 'O enemy of Allah, how dare you speak to the Messenger of Allah like that within earshot of me? By Allah, had I not feared the disintegration of [the treaty between us] I would have surely smote your head with my sword!' This whole time the Messenger of Allah ﷺ was looking at ʿUmar with tranquility and deliberation, and was smiling. Then he ﷺ said, 'He and I are more in need of something else from you, ʿUmar. Tell me to pay him what he is owed, and tell him to seek what he is owed in a well-mannered way. Go with him and give him what he is owed and add twenty *ṣāʿ*s to it for having frightened him.' ʿUmar did as he was told. I then said to ʿUmar, 'I have come to recognize all but two of the signs of prophethood in the face of the Messenger of Allah ﷺ when I looked upon him. There remained but two signs which I had yet to test out: that his forbearance overcomes his anger, and that extreme ignorance only increases him in forbearance. I tested him, and lo I call you to bear witness that I am pleased with Allah as my Lord, with Islam as my religion, and with Muḥammad ﷺ as my Prophet!'"

Qāḍī ʿIyāḍ said in *al-Shifā*:

> What we have mentioned from the rigorously authenticated collections and sound compilations of hadith (whose mass-transmitted reports have reached the degree of certainty) should suffice you in recognizing the Prophet's patience in the face of the harshness of Quraysh and the injuries suf-

fered in the period of ignorance, and his endurance in the face of severe difficulties with them—until Allah Most gave him victory over them (with the conquest of Mecca) and they had no doubt that they would be wiped out and decimated, but he did nothing but pardon and forgive them. He asked them, "What do you think I shall do to you?" and they replied, "You shall do what is good, O noble brother, son of a noble brother!" He ﷺ said to them, "Go, for you are freed!"

Anas ﷺ related, "Some eighty men from Tanᶜīm[600] came to the Dawn Prayer to assassinate the Messenger of Allah ﷺ but they were apprehended. The Messenger of Allah ﷺ set all of them free, whereupon Allah revealed, '*And it is He who restrained their hands from you, and your hands from them, in the midst of Mecca, after He gave you victory over them. And Allah see all that you do.*'" (Quran 48:24)[601]

When Abū Sufyān was brought to the Prophet ﷺ after rousing the Confederates against him and killing his uncle and Companions and mutilating their bodies, the Prophet ﷺ pardoned him and spoke gently with him and said, "Be of good cheer, Abū Sufyān. Has not the time come for you to acknowledge that there is no god but Allah?" Abū Sufyān replied, "May my father and mother be sacrificed for you! How forbearing you are! How strong your filial piety! How generous you are!"[602]

600 A place some eight miles outside of Mecca. [t]
601 Muslim, *Ṣaḥīḥ*.
602 Al-Ṭabarānī, *al-Muᶜjam al-kabīr*.

Al-Nawawī said in *Tahdhīb* [*al-asmā' wa al-lughāt*]:

Allah (Glorified and Exalted is He!) has gathered for the Prophet ﷺ perfect qualities of character and beautiful morals, and has given him the knowledge of the first and the last [nations], and knowledge that occasions salvation and triumph—even though he is unlettered, without reading or writing, and without a human teacher. He has given him what He has given to no other among creation, and He has chosen him over the first and the last. He gave him all of the keys to the treasures of the earth but he refused and chose the Hereafter over them. He was as Allah Most High described him: "*Certainly there has come to you a Messenger from your own selves. It grieves him that you should suffer. He is keen for you* [your well-being], *and with the believers he is full of pity, merciful.*" (Quran 9:128)

SECTION TWO

The Description of the Prophet's ﷺ Companionship with His Wives (may Allah be pleased with them all)

WHEN THE MESSENGER of Allah ﷺ was alone with his wives he was the softest and most generous of people, and he would laugh and smile.[603]

The Messenger of Allah ﷺ was the merriest (*afkah*) of people.[604] Al-Munāwī said, "This means he would joke more than others when he was alone with his family and the like."

ʿĀʾisha ﷺ reported, "The Messenger of Allah ﷺ narrated a story one night to his wives. One of them commented, 'It is as if it is the story of Khurāfa.' He asked, 'Do you know who Khurāfa is? He was a man from Banū ʿUdhra who was captured by jinns in the period of ignorance. He remained with them for a period of time until they returned him to [his fellow] humans. He would narrate to the people the oddities that he saw, and because of that the people began to say "The story of Khurāfa."'"[605]

603 Al-Muttaqī al-Hindī, *Kanz al-ʿummāl*.
604 Ibn ʿAsākir, *Tārīkh Dimashq*.
605 Al-Tirmidhī, *Shamāʾil*.

The Messenger of Allah ﷺ would often kiss his daughter Fāṭima on the top of her head, and would often kiss her mouth.[606]

The Messenger of Allah ﷺ, when among his Companions and wives, was like one of them, and his companionship was excellent. ʿĀʾisha ؓ would say, "When I would desire a thing, the Prophet ﷺ would meet my want." [She also said] "When I would drink from a utensil, he would take it and place his mouth over the part my mouth touched and drink from that spot."[607] [She also said] "He would take my left-over meat on the bone and bite it."[608] [She also said] "He would recline in my lap and recite the Quran."[609]

ʿĀʾisha ؓ told the Messenger of Allah ﷺ the story of Umm Zaraʿ, who was one of a group of eleven women [in the period of ignorance] who took a solemn oath among themselves that they would not conceal anything about their husbands. Each woman described her husband, and the best of them at describing her husband and the one who detailed the most good qualities of her husband was the wife of Abū Zaraʿ. ʿĀʾisha ؓ said, "The Messenger of Allah ﷺ said to me, 'I am unto you as Abū Zaraʿ was unto Umm Zaraʿ.'"[610]

The Messenger of Allah ﷺ would send ʿĀʾisha ؓ to go and play with some of the girls of the Helpers.[611] He would also show her the Abyssinians as they played

606 Ibn ʿAsākir, *Tārīkh Dimashq*.
607 Muslim, *Ṣaḥīḥ*.
608 Ibid.
609 Agreed upon.
610 Al-Tirmidhī, *Shamāʾil*.
611 Agreed upon.

inside the Mosque, and she would lean on his shoulder.[612] It is also related that the Messenger of Allah ﷺ raced ʿĀʾisha and she beat him, and then sometime later they raced again and he beat her, and said "This one for that!"[613]

Anas ﷺ said that one day, as they were in the company of the Messenger of Allah ﷺ in ʿĀʾisha's house ﷺ, a large bowl of bread and meat was sent from the house of Umm Salama. The bowl was placed before the Messenger of Allah ﷺ and he said, "Eat," and the Prophet of Allah put his hand inside the bowl and then we did the same. We began to eat. Meanwhile, ʿĀʾisha was preparing a meal in a hurried manner. She had seen the bowl that was brought, and when she finished preparing her meal she went over, placed her meal down [for us] and picked up Umm Salama's bowl and broke it. The Messenger of Allah ﷺ said, "Eat with the name of Allah; your Mother became jealous!" Then he gave the bowl back to Umm Salama and said, "Food in place of food, and a utensil in place of a utensil." This was narrated by al-Ṭabarānī in [*al-Muʿjam*] *al-ṣaghīr*.

In al-Bukhārī's version it reads: "The Prophet ﷺ was once with some of his wives and one of the Mothers of the Believers sent someone to fetch a large container with food. The wife whose house the Prophet ﷺ was in struck the hand of the servant who brought the food, causing the container to fall down and split into pieces. The Prophet ﷺ gathered the broken pieces and put the spilled food back into it, saying, 'Your mother was jealous.' Then he instructed the servant to wait until a container was brought from the wife in whose house he was, and then he gave the unbroken container to the wife whose

612 Al-Bukhārī, *Ṣaḥīḥ*.

613 Abū Dāwūd, *Sunan*.

original container was broken and he left the broken one in the house of the wife who broke it."

ʿĀʾisha ﷺ related, "One day I went to the Prophet ﷺ with some *khazīra*[614] I had cooked for him. I said to Sawda as the Prophet ﷺ was in our midst, 'Eat,' but she refused. I said to her again, 'Eat,' but she refused. Then I said to her 'Eat, or I will toss it in your face!' but she still refused, so I put my hand in the *khazīra* and tossed some in her face, whereupon the Messenger of Allah ﷺ smiled."

When ʿĀʾisha ﷺ would become angry, the Messenger of Allah ﷺ would rub her nose and say, "O ʿUwaysh (little ʿĀʾisha)[615], say 'O Allah, Lord of Muḥammad, forgive me my sin, remove the rage in my heart, and deliver me from the misguiding tribulations.'"[616]

When the Messenger of Allah ﷺ would receive a gift he would say, "Take this to the house of so-and-so, for she was a friend of Khadīja and loved her."[617]

ʿĀʾisha ﷺ said, "Never did I feel jealous of any woman as I was jealous of Khadīja ﷺ. I used to hear him mention her, and he would slaughter a sheep and distribute its meat among her old friends. One day her sister[618] sought permission to visit and the Prophet ﷺ was at ease with her.[619] Then another woman entered, whereupon he

614 *Khazīra* is made by cutting meat into small pieces and pouring water on them and grinding them up and mixing them with flour and clarified butter. [t]

615 A diminutive form of the name ʿĀʾisha. [t]

616 Ibn al-Sunnī, *ʿAmal al-yawm wa al-layla.*

617 Al-Bukhārī, *al-Adab al-mufrad.*

618 Hāla b. Khuwaylid. [t]

619 That is, he ﷺ was happy to see her and welcomed her and made her feel comfortable. [t]

became joyful and inquired about her well-being in the best of manners.[620] After she left he said, 'She used to visit us when Khadīja was alive. Indeed, looking after[621] old friends is a quality of faith.'"[622]

Al-Qasṭalānī said:

> This is how the Prophet ﷺ was with his wives. He would excuse them and not take them to task, and yet if the scales of justice weighed against them he would uphold justice without apprehension or anger. Thus, whosoever contemplates the conduct of the Prophet ﷺ with his family and Companions, and with others among the poor, the orphans, the widows, the guests, and the indigent, will come to realize that his heart reached the pinnacle of sensitivity and softness that no creature has any hope of attaining—and yet with that he was strict to uphold the limits set by Allah as well as Allah's rights and religion, to the extent that he would cut off the hand of the thief, and so on.

620 That is, he asked her how she was doing and inquired about her condition and well-being. [t]

621 The word used by the Prophet ﷺ, *ʿahd*, carries a variety of meanings. According to al-Ḥāfiẓ al-Sakhāwī, it means to tend to and care for something, or to uphold and maintain covenants and agreements made in the past. The meaning here, as reflected in the translation, is to continually look after the well-being of old friends. [t]

622 Al-Ḥākim, *al-Mustadrak*.

SECTION THREE

The Description of the Prophet's Trustworthiness & Truthfulness ﷺ

THE MESSENGER OF Allah ﷺ was, from day one, the most trustworthy of all mankind and the most truthful of them in speech. Allah Most High said, "[He is] obeyed and trustworthy." (Quran 81:21) Most of the scholars of Quranic exegesis maintain that this refers to the Prophet Muḥammad ﷺ. Before he was tasked with the prophetic mission (*nubuwwa*) Quraysh would call him al-Amīn (the Trustworthy).

When [Quraysh] rebuilt the Kaʿba and fell into disagreement over who should reset the Black Stone [in its corner], they agreed to submit to the judgment of the first person to enter the sanctuary after them. Lo and behold, the Prophet entered after them. This occurred before he was tasked with the prophetic mission, and Quraysh said after he entered, "This is Muḥammad the Trustworthy, we are satisfied with his judgment!"[623]

The Prophet ﷺ said of himself, "By Allah, I am the Trustworthy in the sight of those in the heavens, and the Trustworthy in the sight of those in the earth."[624]

It is reported that Abū Jahl said to the Prophet ﷺ,

623 Aḥmad, *Musnad*.

624 Ibn Abī Shayba, *Muṣannaf*.

"We do not consider you a liar, nor do we consider you mendacious, rather we deny what you have brought." After he said this, Allah revealed "*For verily they do not deny you, but rather the wrongdoers deny the signs of Allah.*" (Quran 6:33)

It is said that al-Akhnas b. Sharīq met up with Abū Jahl during the Battle of Badr and said, "Abū al-Ḥakam! There is none but you and I to hear our words; tell me about Muḥammad—is he truthful or is he a liar?" Abū Jahl said, "By Allah, Muḥammad is certainly truthful—Muḥammad has never told a lie!"[625]

Heraclius[626] asked Abū Sufyān about the Prophet ﷺ, "Did you all ever accuse him of telling lies before he proclaimed [prophecy]?" Abū Sufyān replied, "No."[627]

Al-Naḍr b. al-Ḥārith said to Quraysh, "Muḥammad was a young man among you and he was the most accepted among you, the truest of you in speech, and the greatest of you in keeping trusts—but then, when you saw gray hair on his temples[628] and he came to you with the message he brought, you turn around and call him a sorcerer! No, by Allah, he is no sorcerer!"[629]

In the hadith of ʿAlī ؓ the Prophet ﷺ is described as "the truest of men in speech."[630]

625 Al-Ṭabarānī, *al-Muʿjam al-awsaṭ*.
626 The Byzantine emperor. [t]
627 Al-Bukhārī, *Ṣaḥīḥ*.
628 This being a metaphor for maturity, since the Prophet ﷺ received revelation at the age of forty. [t]
629 Ibn Isḥāq, *Sīra*.
630 Al-Tirmidhī, *Shamāʾil*.

SECTION FOUR

The Description of the Prophet's Shyness & Joking ﷺ

Abū Saᶜīd al-Khudrī reported, "The Messenger of Allah was shyer than a maiden in her chamber."[631] When the Messenger of Allah ﷺ disliked something it could be visibly recognized in his face.[632] He ﷺ was the shyest of men and did not stare into anyone's face.[633] Whenever he had to speak about something he disliked, he would speak metonymically to allude to it.[634]

When the Messenger of Allah ﷺ went out to answer the call of nature he would go out for some distance.[635] When he ﷺ wanted to answer the call of nature he would not lift up his garment until he lowered himself[636] closer to the ground.[637]

631 Agreed upon.
632 That is because his face was so luminous, and because he was shy to express his distaste. [t]
633 Qāḍī ᶜIyāḍ, *al-Shifā*.
634 Ibid.
635 Ibn Mājah, *Sunan*.
636 That is, because of the Prophet's shyness ﷺ he would not lift his garments to expose his private areas, even when answering the call of nature. Instead, he would lower himself to the ground in a squatting position and then move his clothes. [t]
637 Al-Tirmidhī, *al-Jāmiᶜ*.

When he would enter the privy, he would put on his shoes and cover his head.[638]

ʿĀʾisha ﷺ said, "I never saw the private parts of the Messenger of Allah ﷺ."[639]

As for the joking of the Messenger of Allah ﷺ, he would joke with women and children and others, but would only say what is true.[640]

The Messenger of Allah ﷺ was the merriest of people with children.[641]

When the Messenger of Allah ﷺ would joke he would lower his gaze.

The Messenger of Allah ﷺ was at times playful.[642]

Anas ﷺ reported that the Prophet ﷺ said to him, "O possessor of two ears!"[643]—joking with him.[644] Anas also reported, "The Messenger of Allah would interact with us, even once saying to a brother of mine, 'O Abū ʿUmayr, what did the *nughayr*[645] do?"[646]

Abū ʿĪsā al-Tirmidhī said:

638 Ibn Saʿd, *Ṭabaqāt*.

639 Al-Tirmidhī, *Shamāʾil*.

640 Al-Shaʿrānī, *Kashf al-ghumma*.

641 Al-Ṭabarānī, *al-Muʿjam al-ṣaghīr*.

642 Ibn ʿAsākir, *Tārīkh Dimashq*. Commentators say that this narration means the Prophet ﷺ would engage in playful jokes and levity to express his love and show that it is permitted in the law. [t]

643 In other words, the Prophet ﷺ was praising him for his keenness of hearing. [t]

644 Al-Tirmidhī, *Shamāʾil*.

645 Commentators say that the *nughayr* is a small bird resembling a sparrow and with a red beak. [t]

646 Al-Tirmidhī, *Shamāʾil*.

The understanding derived from this hadith is that the Prophet ﷺ would joke. It also shows that he would give young children agnomens, as he said to the boy "O Abū ʿUmayr!" It also shows that there is nothing wrong with giving a child a bird to play with.[647] The reason why the Prophet ﷺ said to the boy "O Abū ʿUmayr, what did the *nughayr* do?" is because he had a *nughayr* that he played with but which had died, saddening him, and thus the Prophet ﷺ joked with him and said "O Abū ʿUmayr, what did the *nughayr* do?"[648]

Abū Hurayra ﷺ reported, "They [the Companions] asked, 'Do you joke with us, O Messenger of Allah?' He replied, 'Yes; however, I speak naught but the truth.'"[649]

Anas ﷺ reported, "A man once asked the Messenger of Allah ﷺ for a mount and the Messenger of Allah said to him, 'I will give you the child of a she-camel as a mount.' The man said, 'O Messenger of Allah! What am I going to do with the child of a she-camel?' The Messenger of Allah ﷺ replied, 'Do not all she-camels give birth to camels?'"[650]

Anas ﷺ also reported, "There was a man from the Bedouins named Zāhir[651] who would gift the Prophet ﷺ things from the desert, and the Prophet ﷺ would give him supplies when he wanted to leave. The Prophet ﷺ said of him, 'Zāhir is our companion of the desert and

647 That is, so long as it is played with and not tormented. If the creature will be tormented it is unlawful to allow the child access to it, since it is prohibited to torment animals. (al-Nabahānī)

648 Al-Tirmidhī, *Shamāʾil*.

649 Ibid.

650 Ibid.

651 Zāhir b. Ḥarām al-Ashjaʿī.

we are his companion of the city.' The Prophet ﷺ loved him dearly. Now, Zāhir was an ugly man, and one day the Prophet ﷺ approached him as he was selling his wares in the marketplace. He went behind Zāhir and embraced him. Zāhir, unable to see who it was, cried out, 'Who are you? Let me go!' He then turned around and saw that it was the Prophet ﷺ, and tried his best to rub his back on the Prophet's chest ﷺ. The Prophet ﷺ then began to call out, 'Who will purchase this slave?' Zāhir said, 'O Messenger of Allah! You will find that I am valueless.' The Prophet ﷺ said, 'Nay, in the sight of Allah you are not valueless' or he said 'Nay, in the sight of Allah you are expensive!'"[652]

Zayd b. Aslam ﷺ reported that there was a man who would gift the Prophet ﷺ container of clarified butter and honey, yet when his debtor would come to him seeking payment he would go to the Prophet ﷺ and say, "Give this man the right of his wares!" The Prophet ﷺ would simply smile and instruct someone to pay him the price of the dish.[653] Another narration has it, "Never did fine wares enter Medina except that he would purchase some of them. He would then go [with an item he purchased] and say, 'O Messenger of Allah, this is a gift for you!' But when the seller came and demanded payment from him he would go to the Messenger of Allah and say, 'Pay him his price!' The Messenger of Allah ﷺ would ask, 'Did you not give it to me as a gift?' He would say, 'I do not have the money to pay for it,' whereupon the Messenger of Allah would laugh and instruct someone to pay the seller what he was owed."

652 Al-Tirmidhī, *Shamāʾil.*
653 Abū Yaʿlā, *Musnad.*

Al-Ḥasan [al-Baṣrī] ؓ related, "An elderly woman came to the Prophet ﷺ and said, 'O Messenger of Allah, pray to Allah that He enters me into Paradise.' The Prophet ﷺ replied, 'O mother of so-and-so, no elderly woman shall enter Paradise.' The woman turned to go and began to weep. The Prophet ﷺ said, 'Inform her that she will not enter Paradise as an elderly woman, for Allah says "*We have created them in a new creation, and made them virgins—as beloveds, equal in age.*"'"[654] (Quran 56:35–37)

654 Al-Tirmidhī, *Shamā'il.*

SECTION FIVE

The Description of the Prophet's Humility, Sitting, & Reclining ﷺ

THE MESSENGER OF Allah ﷺ was the humblest of people and the most reposed, but without insolence, and he was the most eloquent of them, but without prolixity. He had the best countenance and nothing of the ephemeral world awed him.

The Messenger of Allah ﷺ was humble, though without abasement.

ʿUmar b. al-Khaṭṭāb related, "The Messenger of Allah ﷺ said, 'Do not go to excess in praising me[655] as the Christians went to excess in praising [ʿĪsā] the son of Maryam, for I am but a servant. Say: Allah's servant and Messenger.'"[656]

People would not be hindered from seeing the Messenger of Allah ﷺ or be pushed away from him.[657]

No one, whether freeman, slave, slave-girl, or pauper, would come to the Messenger of Allah ﷺ for a need

655 That is, one should not go to excess in praising the Prophet ﷺ whereby he ascribes divinity to him or calls him Allah's son as the Christians did with Prophet ʿĪsā . [t]

656 Ibid.

657 Al-Ṭabarānī, *al-Muʿjam al-kabīr*.

except that he would get up and go with him or her and fulfil the need.[658]

The Messenger of Allah ﷺ was not too proud to accept the invitation of a slave woman or pauper.[659]

The Messenger of Allah ﷺ would engage in much invocation [of Allah], and would not engage in unbeneficial talk. He would lengthen the prayer and shorten the sermon. He was not too proud to walk with a widow, a pauper, or a slave until he fulfilled their needs.[660]

Anas ﷺ reported, "The slave-women of Medina could take the hand of the Messenger of Allah ﷺ and lead him wherever they wished to go."[661]

Anas ﷺ related, "A woman[662] came to the Prophet ﷺ and said to him, 'I have a need to ask of you.' The Prophet ﷺ said to her, 'Sit on any street of Medina that you wish and I will come and sit with you.'"[663]

When the Messenger of Allah ﷺ would finish leading people in the Dawn Prayer he would turn his face towards them and ask, "Is there any among you who is sick so that I may visit him?" If they replied in the negative he would then ask, "Is there any among you who has a funeral to attend so that I may follow it?" If they replied in the negative he would then ask, "Is there any among you who has seen a dream that he would like to relate to us?"[664]

658 Al-Shaʿrānī, *Kashf al-ghumma*.

659 Ibid.

660 Al-Nasāʾī, *Sunan*.

661 Al-Bukhārī, *Ṣaḥīḥ*.

662 In another narration of this report it says that the woman was mentally unstable. [t]

663 Al-Tirmidhī, *Shamāʾil*.

664 Ibn ʿAsākir, *Tārīkh Dimashq*.

The Messenger of Allah ﷺ would sit on the ground and eat on the ground. He would milk sheep and respond to a slave's invitation to eat barley bread with him.[665]

The Messenger of Allah ﷺ would visit the sick among the poor who were relatively anonymous, and would serve them himself. He would respond to the invitations of those who invited him, whether they were rich or poor, of noble or low pedigree—he never belittled anyone.[666]

The Messenger of Allah ﷺ would respond to invitations to attend wedding feasts, and he would attend funeral processions. He would go and visit the weak among the Muslims and check in on their sick, and attend their funeral processions.

Anas ﷺ related, "The Messenger of Allah ﷺ would visit the sick, attend funeral processions, ride on a donkey, and accept the invitations of slaves. On the day of the siege of Banū Qurayẓa, he ﷺ was riding on a donkey whose rein and saddle were made of palm fiber."[667]

Anas ﷺ also related, "The Messenger of Allah ﷺ was invited to a meal of barley bread and old oil[668] and he accepted the invitation. He had some armor which he had pawned to a Jew and did not find the money to get it back until he passed away."[669]

Anas ﷺ also related, "The Messenger of Allah ﷺ said, 'If the trotter [of a goat or a sheep][670] was gifted to me

665 Al-Baghawī, *Sharḥ al-Sunna*.
666 Al-Shaʿrānī, *Kashf al-ghumma*.
667 Al-Tirmidhī, *Shamāʾil*.
668 The word used here, *al-ihāla al-sanikha*, means old oil whose odor has changed or become slightly rancid due to age. [t]
669 Al-Tirmidhī, *Shamāʾil*.
670 The feet. [t]

I would accept it, and if I was invited to partake of it I would accept the invitation.'"[671]

Anas ﷺ also related, "The Messenger of Allah ﷺ performed the Ḥajj while riding [a mount with] a dry and worn out saddle topped with a threadbare woolen blanket worth less than four dirhams. He supplicated, 'O Allah, make it a Ḥajj free of ostentation or seeking to be heard[672].'"[673] Despite the Prophet's humility ﷺ, the earth was opened up for him and in that Ḥajj he gifted one hundred camels. When Mecca was opened for the Prophet ﷺ and he entered it with the Muslim armies, out of humility before Allah he lowered his head on his mount till it nearly touched the front part of the saddle.

The Messenger of Allah ﷺ would ride on whatever mount was available to him. Sometimes he would ride on a horse, sometimes a male camel, sometimes a mule, and sometimes a donkey. On other occasions he would walk on foot, barefoot without a cloak or a cap (*qalansuwa*), going out to visit the sick on the outskirts of Medina.[674]

The Messenger of Allah ﷺ would sometimes ride on a donkey barebacked without a saddle. He ﷺ would ride a horse fully saddled; sometimes, however, he would ride it barebacked, and on occasion he would gallop off with it.[675]

671 Al-Tirmidhī, *Shamāʾil*.
672 "Seeking to be heard," or *sumʿa*, is the corollary of ostentation. It is to perform a pious action for the sake of gaining a reputation among others, or to speak about it to others for the sake of notoriety. [t]
673 Ibid.
674 Al-Shaʿrānī, *Kashf al-ghumma*.
675 This is narrated in the collections of al-Bukhārī and Mus-

The Messenger of Allah ﷺ would walk to and from the prayer ground on the days of Eid.[676]

When the Messenger of Allah ﷺ would walk he would lean forward slightly.[677]

Jābir ﷺ said, "The Messenger of Allah ﷺ would come [to visit] me and would not be riding on either a mule or a Turkish horse."[678]

The Messenger of Allah ﷺ would mount his servant or others on the same animal behind him, and would at times mount one person in front of him and one person behind him, with himself in the middle.[679]

When the Messenger of Allah ﷺ entered Mecca he was received by Ughaylima b. ʿAbd al-Muṭṭalib and he was carrying one person in front of him and one person behind him [on his mount].[680]

Qays b. Saʿd b. ʿUbāda ﷺ said, "The Messenger of Allah ﷺ visited us, and when he wanted to leave Saʿd brought a donkey and covered its back with a woolen blanket, and then the Messenger of Allah seated himself on it. Saʿd said, 'O Qays, keep the company of

---

lim: Anas ﷺ related, "The Messenger of Allah ﷺ was the best of people, and the most generous and courageous of them. One night the people of Medina were terrified at a loud sound, and when they set out in the direction of the sound [to investigate] the Messenger of Allah ﷺ sufficed them and met them on his way back after going towards the sound ahead of them. He went to investigate [the sound] while riding the horse of Abū Ṭālḥa without a saddle and with a sword slung around his neck. He said 'Fear not.'" [t]

676 Ibn Mājah, *Sunan*.

677 Al-Munāwī, *Kunūz al-ḥaqāʾiq*.

678 Al-Tirmidhī, *Shamāʾil*.

679 Al-Shaʿrānī, *Kashf al-ghumma*.

680 Al-Bukhārī, *Ṣaḥīḥ*.

the Messenger of Allah [ﷺ].' The Messenger of Allah ﷺ then said to me 'Ride' but I refused.[681] Then he said, 'You either ride or you go back' so I chose to go back."[682] Another narration has it, "Ride in front of me, for the owner of the mount has more right to sit in the front."

In *al-Mawāhib* there is a narration from al-Muḥibb al-Ṭabarī, who relates that the Prophet ﷺ rode a barebacked donkey to Qubāʾ with Abū Hurayra accompanying him. He ﷺ said, "O Abū Hurayra, shall I carry you?" "As you like, O Messenger of Allah," said Abū Hurayra. The Messenger of Allah said, "Get on." Abū Hurayra jumped up to get on but was unable, so he grabbed onto the Messenger of Allah ﷺ and both of them fell off. The Messenger of Allah ﷺ re-mounted and said, "O Abū Hurayra, shall I carry you?" "As you like, O Messenger of Allah," said Abū Hurayra. The Messenger of Allah said, "Get on" but Abū Hurayra was [still] unable, so he held onto the Messenger of Allah ﷺ [in an attempt to mount] and both of them fell off again. The Messenger of Allah ﷺ asked again, "O Abū Hurayra, shall I carry you?" but Abū Hurayra replied, "No, by the One who sent you with the truth, I will not make you fall off a third time!"

Al-Muḥibb al-Ṭabarī also related that the Prophet ﷺ was once on a journey and ordered his companions to prepare a lamb [for a meal]. One man said, "O Messenger of Allah, I will slaughter it." Another man said, "O Messenger of Allah, I will skin it." Another man said, "O Messenger of Allah, I will cook it." The Messenger of Allah ﷺ said, "I will gather the firewood." They protested, "O Messenger

681 Qays refused as a matter of propriety with the Prophet ﷺ, not to disobey him. [t]
682 Abū Dāwūd, *Sunan*.

of Allah we will suffice you from needing to do any work!" The Messenger of Allah replied, "I know that you will suffice me from needing to do any work, but I dislike that I should be set apart in distinction amongst you. Verily Allah, Exalted is He, dislikes to see His servant set apart in distinction amongst his companions."[683]

[Qāḍī ʿIyāḍ] recorded in *al-Shifā*, on the authority of Abū Qatāda ﷺ who said, "A delegation of the Negus [of Abyssinia] came and the Prophet ﷺ stood up to serve them personally. One of his Companions said to him, 'We can serve them instead.' He replied, 'They honored our companions so I love that I should reciprocate the honor.'"

When his sister from wet-nursing, Shaymāʾ, was brought among the captives of Hawāzin and she made herself known to him, the Prophet ﷺ spread out his cloak for her and said, "If you like, you can remain here with me, honored and loved, or I can give you supplies and you can return to your people." She chose to return to her people, so the Prophet ﷺ provided her with supplies.[684]

Abū Ṭufayl ﷺ said, "I saw the Prophet ﷺ when I was a young boy; a woman came toward him. When she drew near, he spread out a cloak for him and she sat upon

683 This shows the immense humility of the Prophet ﷺ who in reality has the highest distinction of all of Allah's creation. The Prophet ﷺ said in another hadith, "I am the master of the children of Ādam, and that is no boast." Some scholars have commented that the Prophet only conveyed this by Allah's command so we know his lofty station; otherwise, due to his great humility, he would not have spoken about his supreme rank over creation. [t]

684 Qāḍī ʿIyāḍ, *al-Shifā*.

it. I asked, 'Who is this?' and they replied, 'She is his wet-nurse who suckled him.'"[685]

ʿAmr b. al-Sāʾib related, "The Messenger of Allah ﷺ was sitting one day when his father from suckling came to him. The Messenger of Allah ﷺ put out part of his garment for him and he sat upon it. Then came his mother from suckling, and he put out part of his garment on the other side for her and she sat upon it. Then came his brother from suckling, whereupon the Messenger of Allah got up and had him sit in front of him."[686]

The Prophet ﷺ used to send money and clothing to Thuwayba, the emancipated slave-girl of Abū Lahab and his wet-nurse. When she died the Prophet ﷺ asked "Which of her kin are still alive?" and he was told "No one."[687]

The Messenger of Allah ﷺ would seek victory and help through the poor among the Muslims.[688]

The Messenger of Allah ﷺ had male and female slaves, but did not eat finer food or wear better clothes than they.[689]

The Messenger of Allah ﷺ would eat with his servant[690] and would sit with the poor.[691]

685 Ibid.

686 Ibid.

687 Ibid.

688 This means the Prophet ﷺ would seek victory and help through the supplications of the poor among the Muslims, owing to their humility and brokenness. [t]

689 Al-Shaʿrānī, *Kashf al-ghumma*.

690 Abū Bakr al-Ḍaḥḥāk, *Shamāʾil*.

691 Abū Dāwūd, *Sunan*.

The Messenger of Allah ﷺ would eat with the poor and indigent, and would pick out the lice in their garments.[692]

The Messenger of Allah ﷺ would sew his garment, mend his sandals, and do as men do in their homes.[693] ʿĀʾisha ﷺ was asked, "What did the Messenger of Allah ﷺ do around the house?" She replied, "He was a man among men: he would remove anything attached to his garments[694], he would milk his goat, and he would take care of his personal needs."[695]

Anas ﷺ said, "The Messenger of Allah ﷺ was the most cheerful of men in his countenance. When he would enter his home most of his work consisted of sewing. In his home he would do what others did—carrying things in and out, tending to the upkeep of his house, cutting up meat, and helping his servant."[696]

The Messenger of Allah ﷺ would ride on a donkey, mend his sandals, patch up his shirt, and wear woolen garments. He would say, "Whosoever seeks a way other than my Sunna is not from me."[697]

The Messenger of Allah ﷺ would hobble his camel and take it out to graze. He would eat with servants and knead bread with them and carry his goods from the marketplace.[698] Abū Hurayra ﷺ said, "I entered the marketplace with the Messenger of Allah ﷺ and he

692 Al-Shaʿrānī, *Kashf al-ghumma*.
693 Aḥmad, *Musnad*.
694 Such as thorns, straw, or the like. [t]
695 Al-Tirmidhī, *Shamāʾil*.
696 Ibn Saʿd, *Ṭabaqāt*.
697 Ibn ʿAsākir, *Tārīkh Dimashq*.
698 Qāḍī ʿIyāḍ, *al-Shifā*.

purchased a pair of trousers. I went to carry them but he said, 'The owner of something has more right it.'"[699]

Anas ؓ said, "There was no one more beloved to them than the Messenger of Allah ﷺ. When they would see him they would not stand up since they knew he disliked that."[700]

As for the sitting of the Messenger of Allah ﷺ, Khārija b. Zayd ؓ reported, "The Prophet ﷺ was the most dignified person in his gatherings and would seldom move his limbs."[701]

The Prophet's gatherings were gatherings of forbearance and shyness, patience and trust. Voices were not raised, sanctities were not violated, and odious behavior was not displayed. They were equal and only superior to one another on the basis of God-consciousness. They were humble; they would show respect to the elders, have mercy upon the young, give preference to those in need, and look after the strangers. They would enter as seekers and disperse as guides (i.e., to goodness).

The Prophet ﷺ would sit amongst his Companions and intermingle with them as if he was one of them. When a stranger would come he would not know which of them is the Prophet ﷺ until he asked about him. Because of this, the Companions asked the Prophet to sit in such a way that he would be recognized by a stranger, and so they constructed for him a mud bench that he sat upon.[702]

699 Al-ʿUqaylī, *al-Ḍuʿafāʾ*.
700 Al-Tirmidhī, *Shamāʾil*.
701 Qāḍī ʿIyāḍ, *al-Shifā*.
702 Al-Shaʿrānī, *Kashf al-ghumma*.

When the Messenger of Allah ﷺ would sit his Companions would sit around him in circles.

Never did the Messenger of Allah ﷺ spit except that it would land in the hand of a man among his Companions, who would then rub his face and skin with it. And when the Messenger of Allah ﷺ would perform ablutions, they would almost fight one another to get the water that he used for washing. When the Companions would speak in the presence of the Messenger of Allah ﷺ they would lower their voices, and out of reverence for him ﷺ they would not stare directly at him.[703]

The Messenger of Allah ﷺ would give advice and exhortation to his Companions at intervals.[704]

Abū Saʿīd al-Khudrī ؓ said, "When the Messenger of Allah ﷺ would sit in the Mosque he would pull his legs toward his stomach and wrap his arms around them."[705] The word used to describe this manner of sitting, *iḥtibā*, is to sit and pull one's legs close to the stomach and wrap a turban or a similar object around the legs and the back and fasten it.[706] The "arms" [as mentioned in the hadith] are used in place of what can be wrapped around the back and legs, such as a turban.

When sitting, the Messenger of Allah ﷺ would usually sit with his shins together, grasping them like a

703 Al-Bukhārī, *Ṣaḥīḥ*.

704 This is in reference to the hadith of ʿAbdullāh b. Masʿūd in *Ṣāḥīḥ al-Bukhārī*, who said, "The Messenger of Allah ﷺ would deliver exhortations to us in intervals in fear of us becoming bored." [t]

705 Al-Tirmidhī, *Shamāʾil*.

706 That is, to free one's hands from needing to hold the legs close to the stomach. [t]

cloth wrap used for support.[707] His sitting place could not be distinguished from the sitting places of his Companions[708] because "he would sit wherever space remained in the gathering."[709] He was never seen stretching out his legs in the presence of his Companions, lest his legs take up room and make it constricted for them—the exception being when there was ample space with no narrowness.[710] On most occasions, the Messenger of Allah ﷺ sat facing the direction of the prayer (*Qibla*).[711]

Qayla b. Makhrama ﵂ reported that she saw the Messenger of Allah in the Mosque sitting in the *qurfuṣāʾ* position. She said, "When I saw the Messenger of Allah ﷺ sitting in such a humble and tranquil manner I shivered out of awe of him."[712] The *qurfuṣāʾ* position is to sit with one's thighs pulled in toward his stomach while wrapping his arms around his shins. This is the same as the *iḥtibā* position. It is also said that the *qurfuṣāʾ* position is to sit with [one] knee lifted while bringing one's thighs close and wrapping one's arm around [the standing leg].

Anas ﵁ reported, "A man was brought to the Prophet's presence and felt frightened due to his awe, so the Prophet ﷺ said to him, 'Be at ease. I am not a king; I am but a son of a woman from Quraysh who eats cured meat.' The man then spoke of his need, whereupon the Prophet ﷺ stood up and said, 'O people! It has been revealed to me that you must humble yourselves. Humble yourselves so that one does not transgress against anoth-

707 Al-Shaʿrānī, *Kashf al-ghumma*.
708 Al-Nasāʾī, *Sunan*.
709 Al-Tirmidhī, *Shamāʾil*.
710 Ibn Mājah, *Sunan*.
711 Al-Ṭabarānī, *al-Muʿjam al-awsaṭ*.
712 Al-Tirmidhī, *Shamāʾil*.

er, and no one boasts over another. Be you all servants of Allah, brothers!'"[713]

ʿAbdullāh b. Zayd ﷺ reported that he saw the Prophet ﷺ lying down in the Mosque with one leg placed over the other.[714]

Abū Dāwūd narrates with a rigorously authenticated chain of transmission that after the Messenger of Allah ﷺ would pray the Dawn Prayer he would sit and invoke [Allah] until the sun rose fully.

The Messenger of Allah ﷺ would not rise from his gatherings without saying "Glorified and Exalted are You, O Allah, and to You is all praise. There is no god but You. I seek Your forgiveness and repent unto You." He ﷺ said regarding this supplication, "Verily, no one says this when rising from his gathering except that he is forgiven for whatever he did [of sins] in that gathering."[715]

Whenever the Messenger of Allah ﷺ wished to get up from a gathering he would seek forgiveness [of Allah] ten or fifteen times. Ibn al-Sunnī narrates that he would seek forgiveness twenty times.

When the Messenger of Allah ﷺ would complete his prayer, he would turn to his side.[716]

713 Al-Ḥākim, *al-Mustadrak*.
714 Al-Tirmidhī, *Shamāʾil*.
715 Al-Ḥākim, *al-Mustadrak*.
716 Abū Dāwūd, *Sunan*. According to the Ḥanafī school of law it is preferred to turn one's right side to the prayer niche after the closing salutations of the prayer, while according to the Shāfiʿīs it is preferred to turn one's left side to the prayer niche. Some scholars note that despite the difference of opinion over which side should be toward the prayer niche, anyone who leads prayer in the Mosque of the Prophet ﷺ in Medina should turn his right side toward the prayer niche, for if he turns his left side to it he will turning his back toward the Sacred Enclosure where the

When the Messenger of Allah ﷺ would get up he would lean on one of his hands.[717]

As for the reclining of the Messenger of Allah ﷺ, Jābir b. Samura ﷺ reports, "I saw the Messenger of Allah ﷺ reclining on a cushion on his left side."[718] Abū Bakra ﷺ reported, "The Messenger of Allah ﷺ said, 'Shall I not inform you of the gravest of the major sins?' They [the Companions] said, 'Of course, O Messenger of Allah!' He said, 'To associate partners with Allah and to harm one's parents.' The Messenger of Allah ﷺ was reclining but then sat up. Then he said, 'And bearing false witness'—or he said 'uttering a false statement.' He continued repeating the last phrase until we said to ourselves that we wished he would be silent."[719]

Prophet ﷺ is buried. [t]

717 Al-Ṭabarānī, *al-Muʿjam al-kabīr*.

718 Al-Tirmidhī, *Shamāʾil*.

719 Ibid. Abū Bakra's statement "we wished he would be silent" was out of concern for the Messenger of Allah ﷺ, as they did not like to see him displeased. It is also possible that they were afraid that an affliction would descend. [t]

SECTION SIX

The Description of the Prophet's Generosity & Bravery ﷺ

JĀBIR ﵁ REPORTED, "Never was the Messenger of Allah ﷺ asked for something to which he said 'No.'"[720] He ﷺ was never asked for anything but that he gave it[721], after which he would return to his provision for the year and prefer [the seeker over himself], often being in need before the end of the year if nothing came to him.

Seldom was the Messenger of Allah ﷺ asked to do something for someone except that he would do it.[722]

The Messenger of Allah ﷺ would seldom say no. When he was asked to do something and he wanted to do it he would say "Yes," and if he did not want to do it he would simply remain silent.[723]

Ibn ʿAbbās ﵄ reported, "'The Messenger of Allah ﷺ was the most generous of people in goodness. He was most generous during the month of Ramaḍān, when Jibrīl would meet with him and review the Quran. When Jibrīl would meet with him, the Messenger of Allah ﷺ

720 Ibid.
721 Al-Daylamī, *Musnad*.
722 Al-Ṭabarānī, *al-Muʿjam al-kabīr*.
723 Al-Dārimī, *Sunan*.

was more generous with good than a swift breeze."[724]

ʿUmar b. al-Khaṭṭāb ﷺ reported that a man came to the Prophet ﷺ and asked him [for money], to which he said, "I have nothing, but go and purchase [something] in my name, and when something [of wealth] comes to us we will pay its price on your behalf." Upon hearing this, ʿUmar said, "O Messenger of Allah! I have already give him! Allah has not imposed upon you what you cannot do!' But the Prophet ﷺ disliked what ʿUmar said. Then a man from the Helpers said, "Spend, O Messenger of Allah, and fear not reduction of wealth from the Possessor of the Throne [Allah]!" The Messenger of Allah ﷺ then smiled and his happiness with the Helper's statement was visible on his face, and he said, "This is what I have been commanded with."[725]

When wealth would come to the Messenger of Allah ﷺ he would not spend the night or day with it in his possession. That is to say, if wealth came to him at the end of the day he would not keep it in his possession through the night, and if it came to him at the early part of the day he would not keep it in his possession through the time of his siesta; rather, he would hasten to distribute it.[726]

The Messenger of Allah ﷺ was the most generous of men; he never spent the night with a dinar or dirham in his possession. If the night fell suddenly and something extra remained with him and he was unable to find one to whom he could give it, he would not retire to his home until he gave that excess to someone in need of it.[727]

724 Agreed upon.
725 Al-Tirmidhī, *Shamāʾil*.
726 Al-Bayhaqī, *Sunan*.
727 Al-Shaʿrānī, *Kashf al-ghumma*.

A man once came to the Messenger of Allah ﷺ asking him for something, and he gave [a flock of] sheep so large as to close the gap between two mountains. The man returned to his people and said, "Accept Islam, for Muḥammad gives as one who fears not poverty!"[728]

The Messenger of Allah ﷺ would, on more than one occasion, give someone one hundred camels. [In fact], he ﷺ gave Ṣafwān [b. Umayya] three hundred camels.

[Qāḍī ʿIyāḍ said:]

> This was his way ﷺ even before he was tasked with the prophetic message. Waraqa b. Nawfal[729] said to him, "You bear the burdens of all and give [to others] what they cannot find with anyone else." And Khadīja ﷺ said to him, "Be of good cheer, for by Allah, Allah will never disgrace you! You uphold good relations with your kin, you bear the burdens of all and give [to others] what they cannot find with anyone else, and you treat guests generously, and you are given aid in the vicissitudes of fortune."[730]
>
> The Messenger of Allah ﷺ gave al-ʿAbbās so much that he was unable to carry it.[731] On one occasion 90,000 dirhams were brought to the Messenger of Allah ﷺ and placed on a mat, whereupon he stood up and distributed them. He did not turn anyone away until he had given them all away.[732]

728

729 The commentators on Qāḍī ʿIyāḍ's *al-Shifā* note that it was actually Khadīja who said this and not Waraqa. [t]

730 Al-Bukhārī, *Ṣaḥīḥ*.

731 Ibid.

732 Al-Tirmidhī, *al-Jāmiʿ*.

On the Prophet's return from Ḥunayn, Bedouin Arabs came to him and persisted in asking him until they compelled him to climb up a thorny tree, resulting in his cloak being snatched from him. The Messenger of Allah ﷺ then stood up and said, "Give me back my cloak! If I had camels equal to the number of these trees, I would have distributed them amongst you, and you will not find me miserly, a liar, or a coward!"[733]

The Messenger of Allah ﷺ returned the captives of Hawāzin and they were six thousand in number.[734]

[Al-Qasṭalānī] mentions in *al-Mawāhib*:

Ibn al-Fāris said in his book *Asmāʾ al-Nabī* ﷺ (The Names of the Prophet), "On the day of the Battle of Ḥunayn a woman came to the Prophet ﷺ and recited some poetry that reminded him of the time when he suckled with the Hawāzin. He then returned to them what he had taken[735] and gave them ample supplies, valued at five hundred thousand or more."[736] Ibn Diḥya said, "This is the pinnacle of largesse, the like of which is unheard of in creation."

ʿAʾisha ﷺ reported that the Prophet ﷺ would accept gifts and give gifts in return.[737] A woman once came to

733 Al-Bayhaqī, *Dalāʾil al-Nubuwwa*.

734 Qāḍī ʿIyāḍ, *al-Shifā*.

735 Of captives, not spoils, since the spoils were distributed among the soldiers. [t]

736 The literal phrase in the Arabic is five hundred thousand thousand, or five million. [t]

737 Al-Bukhārī, *Ṣaḥīḥ*.

the Messenger of Allah ﷺ with a cloak. She said, "O Messenger of Allah, shall I give it to you for you to wear?" The Messenger of Allah ﷺ was in need of it so he took it from her and put it on. One of the Companions saw him wearing it and said, "O Messenger of Allah, how beautiful this is! Give it to me to wear!" The Messenger of Allah ﷺ said, "Yes." When the Messenger of Allah ﷺ got up his Companions took the man to task and said, "It wasn't right for you to ask the Messenger of Allah ﷺ for his cloak after seeing him in need of it, especially when you know that he does not deny anyone who asks him for something!"[738] This was narrated by al-Bukhārī.

The Messenger of Allah ﷺ was merciful. No one would come to him except that he would promise him something and fulfill his promise to him if he had something in his possession [to give].

As for the bravery of the Messenger of Allah ﷺ, he was the most valorous and bravest of men. ʿAlī ؓ said, "You have indeed seen me during the Battle of Badr when we were seeking refuge in the Prophet ﷺ, who was the closest to the enemy. On that day he was the most courageous of men."[739] ʿAlī also said, "When the heat of battle intensified and the two parties met [in combat], we would seek protection behind the Messenger of Allah ﷺ and there would be no one closer to the enemy than he."[740]

It is said that the Prophet ﷺ spoke little and was few of words, but when he would order the people to

738 Sahl b. Saʿd mentioned that the man replied, "By Allah, I have only asked him so it can be my burial shroud!" [t]

739 Aḥmad, *Musnad*.

740 Ibid.

fight he would go forth resolutely.[741] He was courageous in battle.[742] The brave man would be the one nearest to the Prophet ﷺ since the Prophet was the nearest to the enemy.[743] ʿImrān b. Ḥuṣayn ﷺ said, "The Messenger of Allah ﷺ never came upon a squadron but that he was the first to strike."[744] They said, "He was immensely courageous. When the idol-worshippers surrounded him, he alighted from his mule and cried out:

I am the Prophet; that is no lie!
I am the son of ʿAbd al-Muṭṭālib!

No one witnessed on that day anyone more powerful than him!"[745]

A man asked al-Barāʾ b. [ʿĀzib] ﷺ, "Did you all desert the Messenger of Allah ﷺ during the Battle of Ḥunayn?" Al-Barāʾ replied, "Yes; however, the Messenger of Allah ﷺ did not flee. The Hawāzin were skilled archers. When we met them in battle they fled, so we went to collect the war booty but then they began to shoot arrows at us. I saw the Messenger of Allah on his white mule as Sufyān b. al-Ḥārith was holding its reins, and he was saying:

I am the Prophet; that is no lie!
I am the son of ʿAbd al-Muṭṭālib!

No one witnessed on that day anyone more powerful than him!"[746]

741 Abū al-Shaykh, *Akhlāq al-Nubuwwa.*
742 Aḥmad, *Musnad.*
743 Muslim, *Ṣaḥīḥ.*
744 Abū al-Shaykh, *Akhlāq al-Nubuwwa.*
745 Agreed upon.
746 Al-Bukhārī, *Ṣaḥīḥ.*

Al-ʿAbbās ﵁ reported, "When the Muslims met the disbelievers in battle, the Muslims turned around and fled and fell back, but the Messenger of Allah ﷺ began to spur his mule toward the disbelievers. I was holding the mule's bridle to prevent it from going too fast, and Abū Sufyān was holding its stirrup."[747]

When Ubayy b. Khalaf had been ransomed on the Day of Badr, he said, "I have a horse that I feed several measures[748] of corn daily and I shall kill you while riding on it! The Prophet ﷺ said to him, "I shall kill you if Allah wills." When Ubayy saw the Prophet on the Day of Uḥud, he urged the horse on after the Messenger of Allah ﷺ. Some of the men among the Muslims tried to block his way but the Prophet ﷺ said "Make way for him" and took hold of a spear belonging to al-Ḥarth b. al-Ṣimma, and he shook it in such a way that those around him took flight as flies fly off the back of a camel when it shakes itself. Then the Prophet turned to face Ubayy and pierced him in the neck, causing him to fall from his horse. It was said that he had broken one of his ribs. When he returned to Quraysh he said, "Muḥammad has killed me!" They said, "There is nothing wrong with you at all!" He replied, "Had everyone here received the injury that I have they would all be killed—did he not say 'I shall kill you'? By Allah, had he spat upon me it would have killed me!" Ubayy died in Sarif as the caravan was making its way back to Mecca.[749]

Anas ﵁ reported, "The Messenger of Allah ﷺ was the best of people, and the most generous and courageous of

747 Muslim, *Ṣaḥīḥ*.

748 The word used in this narration is *faraq*, which al-Nabahānī notes is equal to 6.5 kilograms. [t]

749 Ibn Isḥāq, *Sīra*.

them. One night the people of Medina were terrified at a loud sound, and when they set out in the direction of the sound [to investigate] the Messenger of Allah ﷺ met them on the way—having gone to investigate the sound before them—and said to them, 'Fear not, fear not.' He was riding the horse of Abū Ṭālḥa without a saddle and with a sword slung around his neck. He said to them, 'I found this horse to be very fast.'"[750]

This horse's name was Mandūb. In al-Bukhārī's version of this hadith it reads: "The people of Medina were frightened, so the Prophet ﷺ rode a horse belonging to Abū Ṭālḥa and it was slow, or took narrow steps. When the Prophet ﷺ returned he said, 'I found this horse of yours very fast.' After that the horse was unsurpassable in running."

750 Agreed upon.

Chapter Six

THE DESCRIPTION OF THE WORSHIP, PRAYER, FASTING, & RECITATION OF THE MESSENGER OF ALLAH 

SECTION ONE

The Description of the Prophet's Worship & Prayer 

THE MESSENGER OF Allah ﷺ said, "I am the most conscious of you of Allah, and the most intense of you in reverence for Him."[751] In *Ṣaḥīḥ al-Bukhārī* it is recorded that the Messenger of Allah ﷺ said, "I am the most knowledgably of you all regarding Allah, and the most intense of you in reverence to Him." In al-Bukhārī there is also the narration of Abū Hurayra ؓ who reported that the Messenger of Allah ﷺ said, "Had you known what I know you would laugh little and weep much." In *Ṣaḥīḥ Muslim* there is a narration from Anas ؓ who reported that the Messenger of Allah ﷺ said, "By the One in Whose Hand is Muḥammad's soul, had you seen what I have you would laugh little and weep much." The Companions asked, "What did you see, O Messenger of Allah?" He said, "I saw the Garden and the Hellfire."

Al-Mughīra b. Shuʿba and Abū Hurayra ؓ both reported, "The Messenger of Allah ﷺ prayed so long that his feet swelled. He was asked, 'Why do you do this when Allah has forgiven your past and future sins?' He replied, 'Shall I not then be a grateful servant?'"

751 Agreed upon.

Al-Bājūrī said:

> This has long been a problematic issue, as the Prophet ﷺ is infallible and therefore sinless. The best that has been said regarding the matter is that this phrase is akin to the saying "The good deeds of the pious are the sins of those brought near."[752] Because of the weakness of servitude in the face of the sheer magnificence and immensity of Lordship, no one is free of limitation [vis-à-vis the Divine]—and this is so despite the fact that the Prophet ﷺ enjoys the highest of stations and loftiest of degrees when it comes to his worship and obedience of Allah. The Prophet ﷺ said, "Glorified are You and far removed are You from all defects! We have not worshipped You as You truly deserve. I cannot enumerate praises for You; You are as You have praised Yourself." It is for this reason that forgiveness is said to be of two categories. The first is forgiveness for the common folk, which is for them to be pardoned for sins, and the second is forgiveness of the elect, which is for them to be pardoned for falling short [in worshipping Allah as He truly deserves].[753]

Al-Aswad b. Yazīd said, "I asked ʿĀʾisha about the night prayer of the Messenger of Allah ﷺ. She said, 'He would sleep in the first part of the night and then he would rise [for prayer]. When it was just before dawn he would pray the *witr* prayer and then go [back] to his

752 This is a statement of Abū Saʿīd al-Kharrāz, a great spiritual master who died in the year 280 AH. [t]

753 Al-Bājūrī, *Ḥāshiyat*.

bed. If he wished, he would approach his wife.[754] When he would hear the call to prayer he would rise quickly, and if he needed to take a bath after intimate relations he would pour water over his body[755], otherwise he would perform ablutions and leave for the prayer.'"[756]

Ibn ʿAbbās ﷺ reported that he spent a night in the home of his maternal aunt, Maymūna, the Mother of the Believers ﷺ. He said, "I reclined on the width of a cushion as the Messenger of Allah ﷺ reclined on its length. The Messenger of Allah ﷺ slept until half of the night had passed (or a bit before or after a half), and then he woke up and rubbed the effects of sleep from his face and began to recite the last ten verses of the Chapter of Āl ʿImrān, which starts with the verse '*Verily, in the creation of the heavens and the earth...*' After that he went to a water-skin that was hanging and performed his ablutions well[757] and then stood and prayed. I went and stood by his side[758] and he placed his right hand on my head, took hold of my ear, and twisted it.[759] Then he prayed two units of prayer at a time, six times[760], then he

754 That is, have intimate relations. [t]
755 That is, a full bath (*ghusl*). [t]
756 Al-Tirmidhī, *Shamāʾil.*
757 All of the Prophet's ablutions were done well. What Ibn ʿAbbās means is that he performed all of the obligatory and recommended aspects of the ablution, which include washing each limb three times. [t]
758 In other words, he got up, performed ablutions, and joined the Prophet ﷺ in prayer. [t]
759 In another narration it says that "he moved me to his right side." This means that Ibn ʿAbbās was praying on the left side of the Prophet ﷺ and the Prophet wanted him to move to his right side. [t]
760 In other words, the Prophet ﷺ would pray a total of twelve

prayed a single unit (*witr*). After that he reclined until the muezzin came to him, after which he stood again and prayed two light units of prayer and then left to pray the Dawn Prayer."

In *Ṣaḥīḥ* [*al-Bukhārī*] there is a report from Anas ﷺ who said, "The Messenger of Allah ﷺ would perform ablutions for each prayer."[761]

Ibn ʿAbbās ﷺ reported, "The Prophet ﷺ would pray thirteen units of prayer in the night."[762]

ʿĀʾisha ﷺ reported, "When the Prophet ﷺ would not pray in the night, prevented either because of sleep or fatigue, he would pray twelve units in the day."[763]

Abū Hurayra ﷺ reported that the Prophet ﷺ said, "When one of you stands in the night, let him begin his vigil with two light units of prayer."[764]

Zayd b. Khālid al-Juhanī ﷺ said, "I closely observed the prayer of the Messenger of Allah ﷺ. I was laying down around the threshold[765] of the Messenger of Allah

---

units followed by the *witr* prayer. [t]

761 Scholars note that this was the regular practice of the Prophet ﷺ until after the conquest of Mecca, from which point it was seen that he would offer multiple prayers with a single ablution made earlier in the day. Some scholars opined that it was uniquely obligatory upon the Prophet ﷺ to perform ablutions for every prayer and that it was abrogated after the conquest of Mecca. The majority of scholars, however, hold that the Prophet ﷺ performed ablutions before every prayer to show that it is recommended. There is agreement among the jurists that is permissible to offer multiple prayers with a single ablution provided it is not broken. [t]

762 Agreed upon.

763 Al-Tirmidhī, *Shamāʾil*.

764 Ibid.

765 He was lying down either outside the door of the Prophet's

ﷺ: he prayed two light units followed by two long units, two long units, two long units.[766] Then he prayed two units that were less [in length] than the units prior. Then he prayed two units that were less [in length] than the units prior. Then he prayed a single unit (*witr*)—praying thirteen units in total."[767]

Abū Salama b. ʿAbd al-Raḥmān (may Allah have mercy upon him) said that he asked ʿĀʾisha ﷺ, "How was the prayer of the Messenger of Allah ﷺ during Ramaḍān?" She replied, "The Messenger of Allah ﷺ did not increase in Ramaḍān, or any other mouth besides it, beyond eleven units. He would pray four units—and do not ask about their beauty and their length. Then he would pray four [other] units—and do not ask about their beauty and their length. Then he would pray three units. I asked him, 'O Messenger of Allah, do you sleep before you pray *witr*?' He replied, 'O ʿĀʾisha, my eyes sleep but my heart does not sleep.'"[768]

ʿĀʾisha ﷺ also reported that the Messenger of Allah ﷺ would offer eleven units of prayer during the night, one of which was *witr*, and after he was finished he would lie down on his right side.[769]

ʿĀʾisha ﷺ also said, "The Messenger of Allah ﷺ would offer nine units of prayer during the night." [Al-Bājūrī said] this was done occasionally.

---

house, or he was lying outside the opening of the Prophet's tent on a journey. The latter is more likely since the Prophet would have been with one of his wives if inside his home. [t]

766 Shaykh Yūsuf al-Nabahānī: He said "two long units" thrice to emphasize how lengthy they were.

767 Al-Tirmidhī, *Shamāʾil*.

768 Ibid.

769 Ibid.

Ḥudhayfa b. al-Yamān ؓ reported that he once prayed with the Prophet ﷺ during the night. He said, "When he entered the prayer he said 'Allah is the greatest, the Possessor of sovereignty, omnipotence, grandeur, and magnificence.' Then he recited the Chapter of al-Baqara[770] and bowed, and his bowing was like his standing [in length]. He said [in his bowing] 'Glorified is my Lord the Tremendous, glorified is my Lord the Tremendous.' Then he raised his head, and his standing was like his bowing [in length]. He said [in his standing] 'To my Lord is all praise, to my Lord is all praise.' Then he prostrated, and his prostration was like his standing [in length]. He said 'Glorified is my Lord the Most Exalted, glorified is my Lord the Most Exalted.' Then he raised his head, and the position between to the two prostrations was like his prostration [in length]. He said 'O my Lord, forgive me, O my Lord, forgive me.' [He prayed in this manner] reciting the Chapters al-Baqara, Āl ʿImrān, al-Nisāʾ, al-Māʾida (or al-Anʿām)."[771] What this means is that the Prophet ﷺ offered four units of prayer: in the first unit he recited al-Baqara, in the second unit he recited Āl ʿImrān, in the third unit he recited al-Nisāʾ, and in the fourth unit he recited either al-Māʾida or al-Anʿām—as the narrator of this hadith, Shuʿba, was unsure which one it was.

ʿĀʾisha ؓ said, "The Messenger of Allah ﷺ stood in prayer for an entire night reciting a single verse of the Quran."[772]

770 That is, after reading al-Fātiḥa. [t]

771 Al-Tirmidhī, *Shamāʾil*.

772 Ibid. The verse he recited was: "*If You punish them then they are Your servants, and if You forgive them then certainly You are the Almighty, the Wise.*" (5:118)

ʿAbdullāh b. Masʿūd ﷺ said, "I prayed one night with the Messenger of Allah ﷺ. He continued standing in prayer [so long] that I intended something bad." He was asked, "What did you intend to do?" He replied, "I intended to sit down and leave the Messenger of Allah ﷺ."[773]

ʿĀʾisha ﷺ reported, "The Prophet ﷺ would pray whilst sitting, and when thirty or forty verses remained he would stand up and recite them whilst standing, then he would bow and then prostrate, and then he would do the same in the second unit of the prayer."[774]

ʿAbdullāh b. Shaqīq said, "I asked ʿĀʾisha ﷺ about the supererogatory prayers of the Messenger of Allah. She said, 'He would pray long nights standing and long nights sitting. When he would recite while standing he would bow and prostate from the standing position, and when he would recite while sitting he would bow and prostrate from the sitting position.'"[775]

Ḥafṣa ﷺ, the wife of the Prophet ﷺ, said, "The Messenger of Allah ﷺ would pray his supererogatory prayers whilst sitting, and he would recite a Chapter [of the Quran] in a slow, measured pace until it became longer than a Chapter that was [actually] longer than it."[776]

773 Al-Tirmidhī, *Shamāʾil*.

774 Ibid.

775 Ibid.

776 Ibid. The meaning of Ḥafṣa's statement "until it became longer than a Chapter that was [actually] longer than it" is that the Messenger of Allah ﷺ would recite in such a slow, measured pace that a shorter Chapter would take as long to finish as a longer Chapter read at a normal speed. [t]

Umm Salama ؓ said, "By the One in Whose Hand is my soul, the Messenger of Allah ﷺ did not pass away until the majority of his prayers—apart from the obligatory ones—were performed whilst sitting."[777]

ʿĀʾisha ؓ said, "The Messenger of Allah ﷺ never left the night vigil prayer; and if he happened to be sick or fatigued he would pray [it] whilst sitting."[778]

Ibn ʿUmar ؓ said, "I prayed alongside the Messenger of Allah ﷺ: two units before the Noon Prayer (Ẓuhr), two units after it, two units after the Evening Prayer (Maghrib) in his home, and two units after the Night Prayer (ʿIshāʾ) in his home."[779]

Ḥafṣa ؓ said, "The Messenger of Allah ﷺ would offer two light units of prayer after sunrise."[780]

ʿĀʾisha ؓ said, "The Messenger of Allah ﷺ never omitted the two units of prayer before the Dawn Prayer (Fajr), neither when traveling nor when resident, and neither during health nor sickness."[781]

Ibn ʿUmar ؓ said, "I memorized from the Messenger of Allah ﷺ eight units of prayer: two units before the Noon Prayer (Ẓuhr), to units after it, two units after the Evening Prayer (Maghrib), and two units after the Night Prayer (ʿIshāʾ)."[782] Ibn ʿUmar [also] said, "Ḥafṣa told me of two units offered before the Dawn Prayer but I did not see the Prophet ﷺ pray them."

Muʿādha [b. ʿAbdullāh al-ʿAdawiyya] said, "I said to ʿĀʾisha ؓ, 'Did the Prophet ﷺ ever pray the Forenoon

777 Al-Nasāʾī, *Sunan*.

778 Abū Dāwūd, *Sunan*.

779 Al-Tirmidhī, *Shamāʾil*.

780 Ibid.

781 Al-Khaṭīb al-Baghdādī, *Tārīkh Baghdād*.

782 Al-Tirmidhī, *Shamāʾil*.

Prayer (Ḍuḥā)?' She replied, 'Yes, in four units, and he would increase on that as much as Allah willed.'"[783]

Anas ﷺ said, "The Prophet ﷺ would offer six units of the Forenoon Prayer."[784]

Abū Saʿīd al-Khudrī ﷺ said, "The Prophet ﷺ would pray the Forenoon Prayer so often that we would say that he will never leave it, and he would leave the Forenoon Prayer for so long that we would say that he will never pray it."[785]

Abū Ayyūb al-Anṣārī ﷺ related, "The Prophet ﷺ used to consistently offer four units of prayer in the afternoon[786], so I said to him, 'O Messenger of Allah, why do you consistently offer these four units in the afternoon?' He said, 'Indeed, the doors to the heavens are opened in the afternoon and do not close until after the Noon Prayer is prayed, and I love that some good deeds of mine should ascend in that period.' I asked, 'Is there recitation [of the Quran] in each unit?' He replied, 'Yes.' I then asked, 'Is there a closing salutation (*taslīm*) to divide between them?' He replied, 'Yes.'"[787]

Umm Hāniʾ ﷺ related that the Messenger of Allah ﷺ entered her house on the day of the Conquest of Mecca and bathed and then offered eight units of prayer. She said, "I never saw him pray a prayer lighter than them; nevertheless, he completed the bowing and prostration in them."[788]

783 Ibid.
784 Ibid.
785 Ibid.
786 Before the Noon Prayer. [t]
787 Al-Tirmidhī, *Shamāʾil*.
788 Ibid.

Anas ؓ said, "The Messenger of Allah ﷺ was the lightest of people in his prayers, however they were complete."[789]

Abū al-Wāqid al-Laythī ؓ said, "The Messenger of Allah was the lightest of people when leading others in prayer and the longest of people when praying by himself."[790]

ʿAbdullāh b. Saʿd ؓ said, "I asked the Messenger of Allah ﷺ about praying in my home and praying in the mosque. He replied, 'Do you see how close my home is to the mosque? Yet to pray in my home is more beloved to me than to pray in the mosque—except for the obligatory prayer.'"[791] In other words, the Prophet ﷺ preferred to pray voluntary prayers in his home so that blessings encompass his home and his family, and so that the angels to descend and Satan leaves.

Anas ؓ said, "When the cold grew intense the Messenger of Allah ﷺ would offer the prayer early, and when the heat grew intense he would delay the prayer till it cooled down."[792]

Ibn Masʿūd ؓ said, "The Messenger of Allah ﷺ was never in the midst of people who were offering prayers except that his prayers were more than theirs, and he was

789 Muslim, *Ṣaḥīḥ*. Anas ؓ is speaking about the obligatory prayers that the Messenger of Allah ﷺ would lead others in. As for his voluntary prayers, there are many narrations that speak of their length. [t]

790 Aḥmad, *Musnad*.

791 Al-Tirmidhī, *Shamāʾil*.

792 Al-Bukhārī, *Ṣaḥīḥ*. This means that in times of intense cold the Prophet ﷺ would offer the Noon Prayer as soon as its time entered, and in times of intense heat he would delay the Noon Prayer till the heat of the noon dissipated. [t]

never in the midst of people invoking [Allah] except that his invocations were more than theirs."[793]

Ḥudhayfa b. al-Yamān ﷺ said, "When the Messenger of Allah was beset with a difficulty [another narration has it, "was saddened by something"] he would offer prayer."[794]

Anas ﷺ said, "When the Messenger of Allah ﷺ would stop somewhere on a journey he would not leave until he offered two units of prayer."[795]

The Messenger of Allah ﷺ loved to have the Emigrants and Helpers near him during the prayer so they could commit [the prayer] to memory from him.[796]

The tooth-stick and comb of the Messenger of Allah ﷺ were never away from his place of prayer.[797]

Imam Aḥmad, Muslim, Abū Dāwūd, al-Tirmidhī, al-Nasāʾī, and Ibn Mājah all narrate that when the Messenger of Allah ﷺ finished his prayers he would say "I seek Allah's forgiveness" thrice, and then say "O Allah, You are the Flawless (al-Salām) and from You comes peace and safety (*salām*), blessed and exalted are You, O Possessor of Majesty and Honor."

793 Ibn ʿAsākir, *Tārīkh Baghdād*.
794 Aḥmad, *Musnad*.
795 Al-Bayhaqī, *Sunan*.
796 Aḥmad, *Musnad*. This means the Prophet ﷺ liked to have them near so they could learn the details of the prayer and teach those who do not know and pass it on to future generations. [t]
797 Al-Munāwī, *Kanz al-ḥaqāʾiq*.

SECTION TWO

The Description of the Prophet's Fasting ﷺ

ʿABDULLĀH B. SHAQĪQ said, "I asked ʿĀʾisha about the fasting of the Messenger of Allah ﷺ. She said, 'He would fast for so long that we would say "He will continue to fast and will not break it." Then he would abstain from fasting for so long that we would say "He will abstain and not fast." From the time he entered Medina, the Messenger of Allah ﷺ did not fast for an entire month except for Ramaḍān.'"[798]

Anas was asked about the Prophet's fasting ﷺ. He replied, "He would fast for so long that we would think that he did not want to break it, and would abstain from fasting for so long that we would think that he did not want to fast in it [a month]. You would not wish to see him during the night in prayer except that he was in prayer, and you would not wish to see him sleeping during the night except that he would be sleeping."[799]

798 Al-Tirmidhī, *Shamāʾil*.
799 Ibid. The Prophet ﷺ would offer night prayers at different times of the night, so anyone wanting to see him at a specific time might find him sleeping or in prayer. [t]

Umm Salama ﷺ said, "I never saw the Prophet ﷺ fasting two months consecutively except in Shaʿbān and Ramaḍān."[800]

ʿĀʾisha ﷺ said, "I never saw the Messenger of Allah ﷺ fast in a single month more than his fast during the month of Shaʿbān; he would fast during Shaʿbān save a little; he would fast the entire month."[801]

ʿAbdullāh b. Masʿūd ﷺ said, "The Messenger of Allah ﷺ would fast for three days at the beginning of each month and would seldom break his fast on Fridays."[802]

ʿĀʾisha ﷺ said, "The Prophet ﷺ would purposely[803] fast on Mondays and Thursdays."[804]

Abū Hurayra ﷺ reported that the Prophet ﷺ said, "Deeds are presented [before Allah] on Mondays and

800 Ibid.

801 Agreed upon. This somewhat recondite statement of ʿĀʾisha has been interpreted by scholars in a variety of ways. The best interpretation, mentioned by Imam Ibn ʿAbd al-Barr, is that in his earlier years the Prophet ﷺ would fast most of Shaʿbān, and during his later years he would fast all of it. [t]

802 Al-Tirmidhī, *Shamāʾil*. In another hadith the Prophet ﷺ forbade fasting on Fridays unless one has fasted the day before it or intends to fast the day after it. Because of that, the understanding of this narration is that he had fasted the day prior or intended to fast the day after it. Another interpretation is that fasting on Fridays in particular was one of the things uniquely allowed to the Prophet ﷺ. [t]

803 The Arabic word used here, *taḥarrā*, has been interpreted in two ways: 1) that the Prophet ﷺ would eagerly await these two days so he could fast in them, and 2) he would take efforts beforehand to make sure he fasted on these two days. [t]

804 Al-Tirmidhī, *Shamāʾil*.

Thursdays, so I love that my actions are presented while I am fasting."[805]

Abū Hurayra ﷺ also said, "The Messenger of Allah ﷺ would most often fast on Mondays and Thursdays, so he was asked why and he said, 'Deeds are presented [before Allah] every Monday and Thursday and every Muslim is forgiven except two people who forsake one another, about whom [Allah] says [to His angels], "Hold them back until they reconcile with one another."'"[806]

Umm Salama ﷺ said, "The Messenger of Allah ﷺ would most often fast on Saturdays and Sundays. He would say, 'They are festival days of the idol-worshippers, so I like to be different from them.'"[807]

ʿĀʾisha ﷺ said, "In each month the Prophet ﷺ would fast on Saturdays, Sundays, and Mondays, and at the end of each month he would fast on Tuesdays, Wednesdays, and Thursdays."[808]

Muʿādha ﷺ said, "I asked ʿĀʾisha, 'Did the Messenger of Allah ﷺ fast three days out of each month?' She replied, 'Yes,' I asked, 'On which days did he fast?' She replied, 'He did not specify any particular day in which to fast; he would fast in the beginning of the month, the middle of the month, and the end of the month.'"[809]

805 Ibid.
806 Ibn Mājah, *Sunan*.
807 Aḥmad, *Musnad*.
808 Al-Tirmidhī, *al-Jāmiʿ*. Some scholars have said that the Prophet ﷺ fasted on all of these days to show his nation that it is a Sunna to offer voluntary fasts during each day of the week. The reason why he did not fast six days consecutively was to make things easy for his nation, for had he fasted Sunday through Thursday each week it would have been difficult to follow him. [t]
809 Al-Tirmidhī, *Shamāʾil*.

Ibn ʿAbbās ﷺ said, "The Messenger of Allah ﷺ, whether travelling or resident, would never leave off fasting during the White Days (*ayyām al-bīḍ*)."[810] The White Days refer to the thirteenth, fourteenth, and fifteenth of each [lunar] month. They are called the White Days because the full moon appears during them.

ʿĀʾisha ﷺ said, "ʿĀshūrāʾ[811] was a day that Quraysh would fast during the period of ignorance (*jāhiliyya*), and the Messenger of Allah ﷺ would fast during it, too. So when he entered Medina he would fast during ʿĀshūrāʾ and order [others] to fast during it as well. When [fasting in] Ramaḍān was made compulsory it became the obligatory fast and the fasting on ʿĀshūrāʾ was left, so now whosoever would like can fast during it, and whosoever would like can leave it."[812]

ʿAlī ﷺ said, "The Messenger of Allah ﷺ would fast during ʿĀshūrāʾ and instruct [others] *to* fast during it, too."[813]

Ḥafṣa ﷺ said, "The Messenger of Allah ﷺ would fast on the ninth of Dhū al-Ḥijja, the day of ʿĀshūrāʾ, and three days each month: the first Monday of each month, Thursday, and the Monday preceding the last Friday of the month."[814]

Jābir ﷺ said, "The Messenger of Allah ﷺ liked to break his fast with ripened dates (*ruṭab*) as long as they were still fresh, otherwise if there were no ripened dates he would break his fast with dry dates (*tamar*). He

810 Al-Ṭabarānī, *al-Muʿjam al-kabīr*.

811 The tenth of Muḥarram. [t]

812 Al-Tirmidhī, *Shamāʾil*.

813 Aḥmad, *Musnad*. This is understood to be an order of recommendation not an order of obligation. [t]

814 Ibid.

would conclude his meal with them and make them an odd number, three or five or seven."[815]

Anas ﷺ said, "The Messenger of Allah ﷺ liked to break his fast with three dry dates or something untouched by fire."[816] Anas ﷺ also said, "The Messenger of Allah ﷺ break his fast with ripened dates before he offered the prayer; and if there were no ripened dates he would eat dry dates; and if there were no dry dates he would take a few sips of water."[817]

Anas ﷺ also said, "When the Messenger of Allah ﷺ would break his fast with a people he would say, 'May those who are fasting break their fast with you; may the pious eat of your food; and may the angels descend upon you.'"[818] Ibn al-Zubayr ﷺ said, "When the Messenger of Allah ﷺ would break his fast with a people he would say, 'May those who are fasting break their fast with you, and may the angels send prayers upon you.'"[819] Ibn ʿUmar ﷺ said, "When the Messenger of Allah ﷺ would break his fast he would say, 'The thirst has gone, the veins have been moistened, and the reward has been set, Allah willing.'"[820] Muʿādh b. Zuhra said, "When the Messenger of Allah ﷺ would break his fast he would say, 'O Allah, for Your sake I have fasted, and with Your provision I have broken my fast.'"[821] Muʿādh ﷺ [also] said, "When the Messenger of Allah ﷺ would break his fast he would

815 Ibn ʿAsākir, *Tārīkh Dimashq*.
816 Abū Yaʿlā, *Musnad*.
817 Aḥmad, *Musnad*.
818 Ibid.
819 Al-Ṭabarānī, *al-Muʿjam al-kabīr*.
820 Abū Dāwūd, *Sunan*.
821 Ibid.

say, 'All praise is due to Allah who helped me to fast and provided me that with which to break my fast.'"[822] Ibn ʿAbbās ﷺ said, "When the Messenger of Allah ﷺ would break his fast he would say, 'O Allah, for Your sake I have fasted, and with Your provision I have broken my fast, so accept from me—indeed You are the All-Hearing, the All-Knowing.'"[823]

ʿAlqama said, "I asked ʿĀʾisha ﷺ, 'Did the Messenger of Allah ﷺ specify particular days for specific acts [of worship]?' She replied, 'His deeds were continuous—who among you is able to bear what the Messenger of Allah bore?'"[824]

ʿĀʾisha ﷺ said, "The Messenger of Allah ﷺ came to see me while there was a woman in my company. He asked, 'Who is this?' I replied, 'She is So-and-so; she doesn't sleep at night.'[825] The Messenger of Allah ﷺ then said, 'See to it that you do of [righteous] actions what you can bear, for by Allah, Allah does not become bored when you become bored.' The most beloved actions to the Messenger of Allah ﷺ were those which one does consistently."[826]

Abū Ṣāliḥ said, "I asked ʿĀʾisha and Umm Salama ﷺ, 'Which deed was most beloved to the Messenger of Allah?' Both of them replied, 'That which is done consistently, even if it is small.'"[827]

Al-Bukhārī narrated on the authority of ʿĀʾisha ﷺ

822 Ibn al-Sunnī, *ʿAmal al-yawm wa al-layla.*
823 Al-Ṭabarānī, *al-Muʿjam al-kabīr.*
824 Al-Tirmidhī, *Shamāʾil.*
825 That is, she keeps awake in prayer and invocation for the entire night. [t]
826 Al-Tirmidhī, *Shamāʾil.*
827 Ibid.

who said, "The most beloved religion to the Messenger of Allah ﷺ was that which one does consistently."

SECTION THREE

The Description of the Prophet's Recitation ﷺ

ʿAWF B. MĀLIK said, "I was with the Messenger of Allah ﷺ one night. He used the tooth-stick, performed ablutions, and then stood in prayer. I stood with him. He began and [after al-Fātiḥa] started reading the Chapter of al-Baqara. He did not pass a verse mentioning mercy except that he would pause and ask [Allah for mercy], and he did not pass a verse mentioning punishment except that he would pause and ask [Allah for refuge]. Then he bowed and remained bowing for as long as he had stood. He said in his bowing, 'Glorified is the Possessor of omnipotence, sovereignty, grandeur, and magnificence.' Then he prostrated[828] and remained prostrate for as long as he had bowed. He said in his prostration, 'Glorified is the Possessor of omnipotence, sovereignty, grandeur, and magnificence.' Then[829] he recited the Chapter of Āl ʿImrān, and then one Chapter

828 That is, after rising from the bowing position. [t]
829 That is, after rising to the sitting position and prostrating again. [t]

after another[830], praying the same way in each unit."[831]

Ḥudhayfa said, "When the Messenger of Allah passed a verse that would induce fear he would seek refuge [in Allah], and when he passed a verse mentioning mercy he would ask [Allah for it], and when he passed a verse mentioning Allah's transcendence he would glorify Him."[832]

Abū Laylā said, "When the Messenger of Allah passed a verse that mentioned the Hellfire he would say, 'Woe to the denizens of the Hellfire; I seek refuge in Allah from the Hellfire.'"[833]

Yaʿlā b. Mamlak said that he asked Umm Salama about the recitation of the Messenger of Allah and she immediately[834] described his recitation to him in detail, letter by letter.[835]

Qatāda said, "I asked Anas b. Mālik, 'How was the recitation of the Messenger of Allah?' He replied, 'It was prolonged.'"[836]

Umm Salama said, "When reciting, the Prophet would make clear separations [between the vers-

830 That is, he would recite the Chapter of al-Nisāʾ in the third unit and the Chapter of al-Māʾida in the fourth unit, and so on. [t]

831 Al-Tirmidhī, *Shamāʾil.*

832 Aḥmad, *Musnad.*

833 Ibn Qāniʿ, *Muʿjam.*

834 Because she mastered learning the Quran from the Prophet directly. [t]

835 Al-Tirmidhī, *Shamāʾil.* This last phrase, "letter by letter," has two possible meanings: 1) Umm Salama described the Prophet's recitation in detail, or 2) she told him that the Prophet's recitation was in a measured way where every word is articulated fully. [t]

836 Ibid. This means that the Prophet recited the vowels with proper prolongation (*madd*), neither too short nor too long. [t]

es]. He would recite *'All praise is due to Allah, the Lord of the Worlds,'* and pause. Then he would recite *'The Compassionate, the Merciful'* and pause. Then he would recite *'The Master of the Day of Judgment'…*"[837]

ʿAbdullāh b. Qays said, "I asked ʿĀʾisha ﷺ about the recitation of the Prophet ﷺ and whether he did it silently or audibly. She replied, 'He did both. Sometimes he would recite silently and sometimes he would recite audibly.' I said, 'All praise is due to Allah made the matter spacious.'"[838]

Abū Hurayra ﷺ said, "When the Messenger of Allah ﷺ would recite during the night he would at times recite audibly and at times recite silently."[839]

Umm Hāniʾ ﷺ said, "I heard the recitation of the Prophet ﷺ while I was on my bed."[840]

Muʿāwiya b. Qurra said, "I heard ʿAbdullāh b. Mughaffal ﷺ say, 'On the day of the Conquest of Mecca I saw the Prophet ﷺ atop his camel reciting the verse "*Certainly We have given you a manifest victory; that Allah may forgive you past and future sins.*" (Quran 48:1–2) He recited this verse repeatedly. Were it not that people would gather around me I would have demonstrated to you how it sounded.'"[841]

Ibn ʿAbbās ﷺ said, "The Prophet's recitation in his house ﷺ was such that one could hear it in his courtyard."[842] This means that when the Prophet ﷺ would recite in his home it was possible for the members

837 Ibid.
838 Ibid.
839 Abū Dāwūd, *Sunan.*
840 Al-Tirmidhī, *Shamāʾil.*
841 Ibid.
842 Ibid.

of his household to hear him in their courtyard. The sound of his voice did not go past his chambers.

Abū Hurayra said, "When the Messenger of Allah would recite '*Is He, then, not able to bring life to the dead?*' (Quran 75:40) he would say 'Certainly [He is],' and when he would recite '*Is Allah not the Wisest of judges?*' he would say 'Certainly [He is].'"[843]

Ibn ʿAbbās said that when the Messenger of Allah would recite "*Glorify the Name of Your Lord the Most Exalted*" (Quran 87:1) he would say "Glorified is my Lord the Most Exalted."[844] Abū Hurayra [also] said, "When the Messenger of Allah would recite the verse '*not those who have incurred wrath or those astray*' (Quran 1:7) he would say *Āmīn* such that those near in the first row could hear him."[845]

ʿĀʾisha said that the Messenger of Allah would not recite the entire Quran in less than three days.[846] When the Messenger of Allah would complete an entire recitation of the Quran he would gather his family together and supplicate.[847] When he would finish a complete reading he would recite [again] the first five verses of the first part of the Quran.[848]

843 Al-Bayhaqī, *Shuʿab al-īmān*.
844 Aḥmad, *Musnad*.
845 Abū Dāwūd, *Sunan*.
846 Ibn Saʿd, *Ṭabaqāt*.
847 Al-Nawawī, *al-Adhkār*.
848 Al-Dārimī, *Musnad*.

Conclusion

MAY ALLAH SEND prayers upon our Prophet Muḥammad each time he is remembered by the people of remembrance and each time the heedless fail to remember him. May Allah send prayers upon him among the first and the last—with the most superior, most abundant, and purest of prayers He has sent upon any of His creation. May Allah purify us through sending prayers upon him with the best that He has purified any of this nation through prayers upon him. May peace and the mercy and blessings of Allah be upon him, and may Allah reward him on our behalf with the best that He has ever rewarded a Messenger on behalf of his people!

All praises are due to Allah for all of his graces, both those we know and those we do not know, especially the grace of faith and Islam, and the ability to compile this book. I ask Allah, Glorified and Exalted is He, to benefit me by this book and to grant tremendous benefit by it to all who read it among the Muslims—a benefit that remains with us in this life and in the Isthmus realm (*barzakh*), and that does not leave us on the Day of Judgment—by the rank of he who is the best of means unto Him and the closest of the close to Him, His noblest beloved and supreme Messenger, our master Muḥammad, the liege lord of the Messengers, may Allah send prayers and peace upon him and them as well as their noble families and companions!

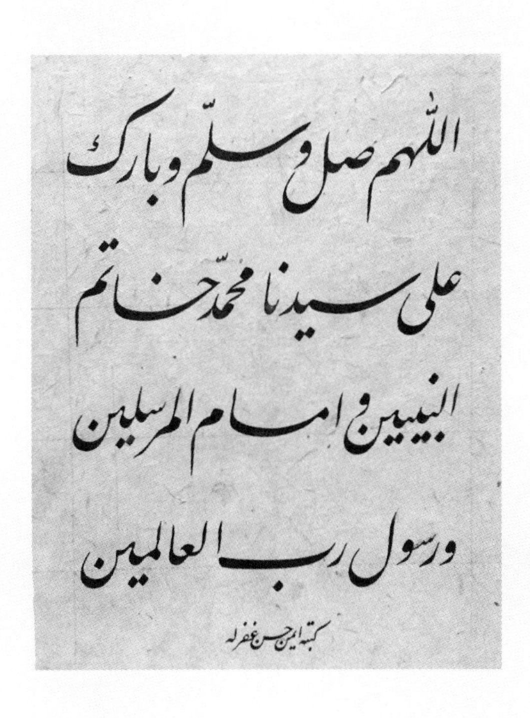

اللهم صل وسلم وبارك
على سيدنا محمد خاتم
النبيين وامام المرسلين
ورسول رب العالمين

O Allah, send prayers, peace, and blessings upon our master Muḥammad, the Seal of the Prophets, the Leader of the Emissaries, and the Messenger of the Lord of the Worlds